Inspirations
for ART

Published by Scholastic Ltd,
Villiers House,
Clarendon Avenue,
Leamington Spa,
Warwickshire CV32 5PR

© 1993 Scholastic Ltd.
Revised edition 1996
1 2 3 4 5 6 7 8 9 0   6 7 8 9 0 1 2 3 4 5

Written by Pauline Kenyon and Tom Reynolds
Edited by Christine Lee
Revised edition edited by Joanne Boden
Series designed by Juanita Puddifoot
Illustrated by Conny Jude
Diagrams by The Drawing Room
Cover design by Micky Pledge
Cover illustration by Rosemary Harris

Designed using Aldus Pagemaker
Processed by Pages Bureau, Leamington Spa
Artwork by Liz Preece, Castle Graphics, Kenilworth
Printed in Great Britain by Ebenezer Baylis & Son, Worcester

British Library Cataloguing in Publication Data
A catalogue record for this book is available from the British Library.

ISBN 0-590-53512-9 2nd revised edition
(ISBN 0-590-53054-2 1st edition)

All rights reserved. This book is sold subject to the condition that it shall not, by way of trade or otherwise, be lent, hired out or otherwise circulated without the publisher's prior consent in any form of binding or cover other than that in which it is published and without a similar condition, including this condition, being imposed upon the subsequent purchaser.
No part of this publication may be reproduced, stored in a retrieval system, or transmitted, in any form or by any means, electronic, mechanical, photocopying, recording or otherwise, without the prior permission of the publisher, except where photocopying for educational purposes within a school or other educational establishment is expressly permitted in the text.

CONTENTS

Introduction		5
Chapter 1	*Drawing and mark-making*	9
Chapter 2	*Painting*	23
Chapter 3	*Printmaking*	35
Chapter 4	*Ceramics*	49
Chapter 5	*Textiles*	59
Chapter 6	*Sculpture*	73
Chapter 7	*Graphics*	79
Chapter 8	*Photography*	87
Chapter 9	*Understanding art and artists*	107
Chapter 10	*Developing the school environment*	133
Chapter 11	*Curriculum planning and assessment*	153
Photocopiable pages		167
Glossary		188
Scottish attainment target chart		190
Resources		191

INTRODUCTION

In the 1995 Statutory Orders for all subjects of the National Curriculum the content and structure of many subjects were significantly revised but art – which must also include craft and design – largely remained the same, although the format was simplified considerably in order to bring a uniform style of presentation across all subjects.

Many teachers who have received specialist art training or who have particular interest and expertise in art, welcome the continued recognition of the important place art has in children's entitlement to a broad and balanced curriculum and they feel eager and excited about its implementation in the busy primary classroom. Many teachers, recognising art as a powerful medium for learning – particularly for young children – are seeking to use some of the unallocated 20% curriculum time identified in the 1995 National Curriculum to give their pupils opportunities to study art in greater depth.

Countless others, although happy that art has received due emphasis, feel concerned at the implications for its delivery and all the necessary areas they need to cover. Moreover, some feel lacking in confidence in tackling the subject at all!

This book is designed to help teachers find confidence and inspiration to teach art, craft and design in their classrooms whilst meeting the demands of the National Curriculum. We hope that both teachers who feel anxious about beginning a more structured approach to art and also more experienced teachers who are seeking to extend their ideas, will find it useful. All the activities featured in the book have been successfully undertaken in schools and there are clear step-by-step explanations of each activity with supporting ideas to help teachers develop tasks further to extend children's learning.

BACKGROUND

All the activities and ideas in this book have been used successfully by the authors or other primary practitioners. We have included illustrations of work wherever possible.

We also hope this book will be useful for teachers who are charged with responsibility for co-ordinating art in their schools. In Chapter Eleven, 'Curriculum planning and assessment' we offer some practical ideas for creating workable policies and guidelines, together with advice on leading colleagues towards the successful delivery of art in the curriculum, including considering resources, strategies for planning, assessment and recording. The National Curriculum for Art makes demands on teachers, of course, but it also places a high emphasis on the development of visual literacy for all children. This is vital as we all live in a world where visual literacy is essential to make sense of and interpret so much that surrounds us – television programmes, films and videos, sophisticated computer graphics, advertisements, photographs, books and manuals, etc. – and also for us to present our own work in an ordered, accurate and dynamic way, ensuring that we express exactly what we intend to demonstrate in

the most effective manner. Teachers are often concerned that the National Curriculum for Art requires two parts of the programmes of study. Investigating and Making and Knowledge and Understanding to be intertwined together. They may feel that a detailed knowledge of art techniques and art history is needed before embarking on the subject. Be reassured that a great knowledge of art and artists is not required to use this book! We have given examples of artists that can be studied to link the two parts of the PoS together – although the suggestions are not exhaustive and there are many other examples that can be used too. The important thing to remember is that teachers can research and learn about a wide range of artists craftspeople and designers and their work alongside the children, making it part of the education process.

We have also included an extensive list of suggested reading which can help teachers learn new techniques or develop existing understanding further, together with a glossary.

The photocopiable section includes pages which we hope will be helpful for children to use in their work and also for assessment and recording purposes.

Many of the ideas and suggestions in this book can be integrated into other areas of the curriculum. However,

Art 7

we want to stress that art should not be seen as merely a 'service industry' to support other subjects but that it is an important subject in its own right, with its own disciplines and formal elements which need addressing and teaching. Children can and do learn through art activities which enrich other areas of the curriculum, but they also need to learn about art and within art. It is important for children to learn specific art skills and develop an understanding of art, including a knowledge of artists from different times and cultures. Many activities in this book have, therefore, been designed to lead on to further developments and activities which will give children opportunities to extend their learning and experience in art. They can also be used separately as appropriate. Teachers can choose to work through particular chapters of activities, building up a repertoire in specific art areas, or they can link work from one medium to another. Suggestions for these links appear throughout the text. Above all, we hope this book will give teachers the opportunity to be flexible in their approach to the subject and to enjoy teaching art to their classes.

CHAPTER 1

Drawing and mark-making

Children – and for that matter adults too – will often say, 'I can't draw!' All too easily children can lose confidence and assume that drawing is something only a few artistically gifted people can do well. This is not the case. Although it is not given to us all to be brilliantly talented and highly acclaimed artists, everyone can learn the skills of drawing.

Moreover, such skills are as necessary as learning to write in a world where there is a real need for planning, problem solving and technological developments; close observation, investigation and scientific progress and new exciting growth in the leisure media/arts industries. Indeed, children will need to draw with confidence and accuracy in order to fulfil many of the requirements of the National Curriculum.

The beauty of drawing, or mark-making, is that there is no right or wrong way! In fact, just like language, there are many uses – and, therefore, many forms and styles – of mark-making. A good analogy would be letter-writing. When we write to our friends we do so in a very different style to the one we use in making a job application, composing a letter of complaint, entering a competition or ordering goods!

Drawing and mark-making 9

BACKGROUND

If we are trying to make an accurate visual record of a building, perhaps as part of a history project, our approach and style will be very different from drawing a plan of that building, or sketching out ideas for making a model of it in scrap materials, or drawing it from memory or even using the imagination to recreate a past scene at the same place, or for preparing an illustration for a book or display. Some types of drawing need to be highly detailed and accurate, whereas those which are trying to convey a general impression will be very free; others will be experimental ideas – reference points to aid thinking and further development.

It is important, therefore, that children have opportunities for work that will enable them to develop these skills and learn to use them appropriately, recognising the different types of drawing – observational, technical/planning and imaginative. They also need to experience challenges which are open-ended and experimental so that they can play with ideas and develop confidence in applying them.

They will need to acquire a vocabulary and an understanding of the conventions of tone, line, shape, pattern and rhythm (the formal elements of art).

Children will need access to a range of materials to help them develop this vocabulary and a bank of skills.

For example, the following items should be available within school:
- a collection of drawing pencils, ranging from 2B to 8B;
- graphite sticks and pencils;
- charcoal;
- pastels;
- felt-tipped pens of varying kinds;
- a range of crayons;
- drawing inks;
- brushes and pens;
- erasers;
- natural marking materials (for example, brick, clay pot, earth, slate, chalk can all be used and form useful links with earth sciences);
- sponges;
- a selection of cartridge papers, ranging in size from A5 to A1;
- a range of other papers including different weights, colours and surfaces;
- a range of other surfaces to draw on (for example, card, tile, slate, wood and pot);
- cheap hair spray (for 'fixing' drawings that smudge easily);
- natural objects (for example, seed heads, stones, skulls and plants);
- 'made' materials (for example, cogs, wheels, glass and plastics);
- a selection of fabrics and textiles.

It is also valuable to have a collection of books, prints, posters and so on which have illustrations of artists' working drawings and planning sketches as well as completed pictures. Some examples of real sketch books would also be very useful. Further details of resources can be found on photocopiable pages 168 to 170.

ACTIVITIES

1. On your marks – 1

Objective
To develop a vocabulary of mark-making through exploration and to introduce tone.

Age range
Three to eleven.

Group size
The whole class.

Time
30 minutes.

What you need
Individual sheets of A4 or A5 paper, a range of drawing pencils (HB, 2B, 3B, 4B and so on) or graphite sticks.

What to do
Ask each child to draw a box approximately 10cm × 2cm, and divide it into five sections, as in Figure 1. There is no need to use rulers.

Ask the children each to use a drawing pencil to shade in the first section as neatly and as darkly as possible. Emphasise using the side of the pencil as well as the point and encourage the use of the whole arm, not only the fingers and wrist. Then ask them to fill in the second section slightly lighter than the first. Ask the children to compare them and note any differences. Encourage the use of appropriate descriptive language, for example, paler, darker, deeper, softer etc.

The third section should be lighter still and again comparisons should be made with the first two sections. Finally let them fill in the two remaining sections with increasing lightness, comparing continually and adjusting if necessary to ensure a progression from darkest to lightest. At this stage you can introduce the word *tone*.

Ask the children to look at their drawing through half-closed eyes and to notice how the darkest tones seem to jump out of the page. Again, encourage the use of descriptive language. Do not rush this exercise – it is vital for further development and lays the foundation for quality drawing work.

If you use graphite sticks children's hands will become beautifully grey – don't panic! It washes off easily with soap and water and the drawing results are worth the effort. However, do warn the children not to lick their hands and ensure that all hands are washed immediately after the lesson.

If you are working with young children or if there is no nearby sink, put a bowl of water on the table and make the cleaning-up part of the process!

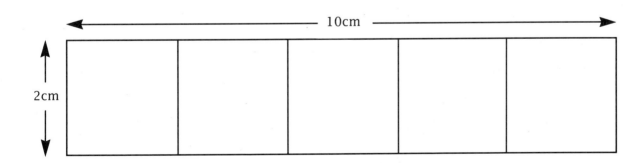

Figure 1

Drawing and mark-making 11

2. On your marks – 2

Objective
To extend the vocabulary of mark-making.

Age range
Three to eleven.

Group size
The whole class.

Time
40 minutes.

What you need
Chalkboard, A4 sheets of white paper, selection of pencils, scissors, paper adhesive, spreaders, cardboard.

What to do
Write on the board a range of descriptive words such as hard, thick, happy, quick, jagged and so on. Ask the children to suggest other descriptive words and to list them.

Give each child a piece of A4 paper and ask them to make a range of marks which illustrate the words. Encourage them to turn their paper round, invent marks and produce light and dark marks (see Activity 1) and to fill the whole paper. Remind them to half close their eyes to check the different tones. Explain that there should be virtually no white paper visible at the end of the exercise and all the words on the board should have been used.

Children can be hesitant to draw freely as they tend to look for 'right answers'. If this happens, ask the children to swap their papers around the class and work on the new one. Discuss, *tone, line, shape, pattern and texture*.

Next, ask the children to cut or tear their sheets into irregular strips. These can be woven, overlaid, intertwined or stuck together to form new two-dimensional structures or even three-dimensional patterns structures on to a base of cardboard.

Further activities
• Divide the paper into irregular shapes as shown in Figure 1 and ask pupils to invent different marks to fill in different areas.
• Let the children use coloured paper and pencils, but limit the choice to one colour only.
Explain that the aim is to concentrate on tone rather than *colour*.

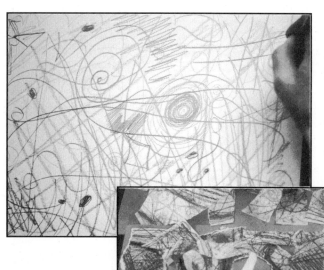

Figure 1

• If possible, show the children some examples of quality drawing. The Leonardo da Vinci drawings are excellent for this purpose, but children will also relate well to the Duhrer drawings (particularly the rabbit). The architectural drawings of the young autistic boy Stephen Wiltshire are particularly useful to demonstrate a range of marks which are stunningly simple yet effective (Resources, page 191).

3. Fingerprints

Objective
To develop the idea of *line* in drawing.

Age range
Three to eleven.

Group size
Whole class (if resources permit) or small groups.

Time
45 minutes.

What you need
A hand magnifying glass for each child, A5 or A4 paper, a range of drawing pencils, an old ink pad or a foam rubber sponge soaked with thick paint, absorbent paper.

What to do
Ask the children to look carefully at their fingertips through the magnifying glasses. Ask them what they notice. Ask them to study all their fingertips and to select one in particular where the fingerprint design is especially interesting. Discuss the total uniqueness of each fingerprint and talk about forensic science and the detection of criminals!

Show the children how to use the magnifiers to help them draw their fingerprints. Children often find this a very difficult thing to do, but when they are sufficiently confident ask them to draw the fingerprint large enough to fill a whole sheet of paper.

Emphasise the need to reproduce the patterns as accurately as possible – it often helps to let them treat the exercise as a forensic detection activity. Ask them to take time and care over their drawing.

While the children are engaged in drawing, circulate and ask them to show you their fingertips and encourage them to describe the shapes. Introduce words such as *arch*, *whorl*, *round*, *spiral* and *curve* to extend their vocabulary.

At the end of the session, let the children compare and discuss their results. Use an ink pad, or a piece of foam rubber soaked with thick paint, to take their fingerprints. Let each child press their fingers gently into the foam just enough to stain their fingertips, then press their fingers on to absorbent paper. Encourage them to compare their fingerprints with their drawings. Let them see how many different patterns they can discover.

Further activity
Let the children paint the designs with bands of different colour following the line of the pattern.

Drawing and mark-making 13

4. Observational drawing

Objective
To develop observational skills and stress the need to look and record what is seen, not imagined.

Age range
Three to eleven.

Group size
Whole class or small groups.

Time
30 minutes.

What you need
A selection of artefacts (such as interestingly shaped objects, kitchen utensils with handles, mechanical objects, shells, musical instruments, flowers etc.), paper or cloth, table, sheets of paper, a selection of drawing pencils, hand magnifying glasses.

What to do
Place the chosen object on a table in good light, standing on a contrasting surface, such as paper or cloth. Let the children sit comfortably around the object, thus giving the class the chance to record the object from a variety of angles.

The difficult part of this activity is preventing the children from rushing to draw without real looking and thinking. Emphasise the need to look carefully before drawing.

The first decision for the children will be to choose either *portrait* or *landscape* formats for their visual record, selecting whichever is the most appropriate for the object and their viewpoint (Figure 1). Encourage the children to use all the paper and consider how the object will be drawn to fill the space. Ask the children to talk about the *shapes*, the *tones*, the *textures* and the relationship of the size and position of the parts of the object to the whole. Encourage the children to study it using the hand magnifiers and note the points of interest – shapes, pattern and detail. The ratio of each part to the whole and to other parts should also be considered. This gives good opportunities for mathematical links, eg. 'How much bigger is the height of the kettle than the length of the spout?'

When the children begin drawing, go round the class, reminding them to concentrate hard and asking questions to challenge their looking and thinking.
- Which direction is the light coming from?
- Which parts are the lightest, darkest?
- Can you invent a mark to show it is a metal object?

Children will often want to rub out lines that they consider 'wrong'. Explain that artists use such lines as reference points. Encourage them to continue drawing and develop their confidence in their use of lines. It is useful to show them examples of

Figure 1

Portrait

Landscape

artist's work where preparation/thinking lines are clearly evident, eg. Leonardo's drawings (cartoons), Henry Moore's sketches etc.

Let the children work for a set period of time and then ask them to stop. Children can then share their work and view each other's drawings. Ask the 'artists' to describe how they are working, the problems they encounter, etc. This forms good links with English work. Either allow the children to recommence work immediately or, if the lesson is timed well, let them enjoy a break/playtime session and return with fresh eyes to resume drawing afterwards. (You may well notice a marked renewal of concentration after a break period.) As a drawing is completed, the 'artist' can talk to the rest of the class about the final work.

Further activity

• Let the children try drawing with ballpoint pens, or with felt-tipped pens.
• Ask the children to arrange the drawings in a row. Ask each child to choose a different drawing (not their own) and describe it ('It is portrait style. It has a lot of detail. Some of the marks are like circles') without indicating the actual drawing. Then ask the group to try to identify the drawing. When they have identified the actual drawing, ask the children if the description was good. Which part of the description, which words, helped you find the correct drawing? How did X describe this part? This should help refine children's selection of descriptive words and improve their 'looking' skills. (These descriptions could be written to go with the drawings on a display.)

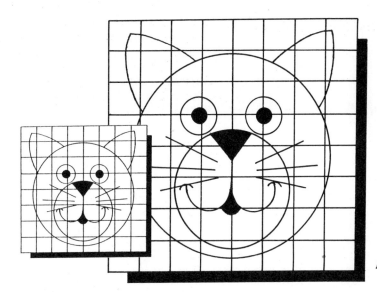

Figure 1

5. Viewfinders

Objective
To increase 'looking' skills.

Age range
Eight to eleven.

Group size
Whole class or small groups.

Time
One and a half hours.

What you need
Viewfinders (strips of black card/paper or pre-cut black paper 'frames' 10cm square), a selection of drawing pencils, sheets of pale coloured sugar paper, previously completed observational drawings.

What to do
Talk to the children about what a viewfinder is used for and show them how it is used. Explain how it is similar to the way in which a photographer uses a camera viewfinder to select an interesting shot.

Let the children arrange the strips to form a viewfinder or use the prepared frame on their drawings, moving them around to find interesting parts.

Discuss the possible choices and encourage the children to choose interesting patterns and shapes rather than very simple lines or too specific details.

When a choice has been made, ask the children to divide the framed section into 16 smaller sections, drawing very faint lines as a guide. Give the children each a sheet of sugar paper larger than the original drawing and show them how it can be 'squared up' to match the shape of the framed area. Ask them to work one square at a time to transfer and enlarge the design as in Figure 1. Explain that the lines should be drawn faintly until any adjustments have been made, then the design can be drawn firmly.

Further activities
• These initial designs can be developed into other media – batik, painting, ceramics, collage etc.
• Let the children print or embroider their designs on to fabric to make a unique record of each individual child's work.

Drawing and mark-making 15

6. Stripes

Objective
To explore line.

Age range
Seven to eleven.

Group size
Whole class or groups.

Time
45 minutes.

What you need
Large pieces of striped material for each child, a range of drawing tools, A4 paper.

What to do
Give each child a piece of striped fabric. It is useful if the pieces of fabric are all different, but it is not essential. Ask the children to describe the features of the material. Prompt them with questions:
• What do you think you would make from this fabric?
• It is natural or synthetic?
• Is the surface shiny or matt?
• What does it feel like?

When they have had sufficient time to examine their fabric, ask them to crumple it up, pleat it or arrange it on the table in front of them in a way that makes the stripes go in a range of different directions. Check that everyone has done this.

Now ask the children to draw their arrangement, concentrating on drawing the lines of the stripes exactly as they appear in front of them. When the children have drawn the initial design, let them change their drawing tools for others that are very different, such as a very soft 6B+ or graphite drawing pencil, or a felt-tipped pen. Ask them to work again on their drawings, emphasising the patterns made by the lines.

7. Portraits

Objective
To develop close observational skills.

Age range
Seven to eleven.

Time
45 minutes.

Group size
Whole class working in pairs.

What you need
A3 paper (both cartridge and coloured papers), a selection of mark-making tools, a selection of reproductions of portraits.

What to do

Show the children some examples of portraits painted by a variety of artists. Good examples are Lowry (*Portrait of the Artist's Mother*; *Portrait of Ann*; *A Manchester Man*; *Head of a Man with Red Eyes*, etc.), the poster portraits of Toulouse-Lautrec, the self-portraits of Vincent Van Gogh, the delightfully busy paintings of Beryl Cook and a range of Picasso's portraits from the gentle *Paul as Harlequin* (1924) to the anguished *Weeping Woman* (1937). Do not show them too many – concentrate on helping the children look closely at individual paintings or drawings.

Focus their thinking by asking them to tell you who they thought the subject was and why the artists painted them. Talk about the differences between posters, self-portraits, imaginative portraits and formal portraits. Discuss together the differences and also the similarities between the examples, concentrating especially on the way the artists have represented the features rather than the way they have used colour. It is possible to form excellent links with English, science, drama and history by asking the children to try to recreate the events which happened just before and just after the portrait was completed. Encourage them to use all the clues they can find from the picture itself.

Arrange the children in pairs sitting opposite each other. Give each pair a piece of paper. If you give out a range of different papers it will make the activity more interesting and extend the learning opportunities as the children compare their results and the effects of different colours and surfaces. Similarly, distribute a varied selection of mark-making tools.

Ask one child in each pair to act as the model for the other and sit very still, full face on or in profile, while the partner draws their portrait. Ask the children to look very carefully and draw only what they see. Prompt them with appropriate questions:
• How far down the face do the eyes come?
• Where is the mouth in relation to the nose and chin?
• What shape and length are the eyebrows?

Emphasise that there are no set rules about the position of features – the exciting thing is that every face is different! Don't rush this activity and encourage the children to spend a longer time looking than drawing.

As each child finishes their portrait, let the pairs change over so that the model becomes the artist.

Leave the portraits on display in the classroom so that the children can study them closely from time to time and then return to their own work.

Further activities

• Use the drawn portraits as working sketches and let the children paint a portrait using the sketches as a reference.
• Ask the children to study carefully one example of a portrait and then create their own drawing in the style of the artist they have chosen.
• Ask the children to draw the back of their partner's head, concentrating on the line and movement of the hair.

8. Self-portraits

Objective
To develop further observational skills.

Age range
Seven to eleven.

Group size
Whole class (if resources permit) or small groups.

Time
45 minutes.

What you need
Examples of self-portraits, A4 paper, a range of drawing pencils or graphite sticks, a mirror for each child.

What to do
Show the children some examples of self-portraits. Discuss how artists use mirrors to help them paint their portraits. Explain how sometimes they make dramatic use of light – perhaps working by lamplight or at particular times of the day to create a special lighting effect.

Let each child have a mirror and ask them to look very carefully at their reflections. Guide their observation with questions to help them make decisions about the relationships of their features.
• Where do the earlobes come to on the side of the face?
• Which is the wider – the forehead or the jawline?
• Are the eyes in a straight line or at an angle?

Ask them to look also at the shapes of features.
• What shape is your face?
• Look at the mouth; are both sides exactly the same?

Allow plenty of time for this part of the activity because you are encouraging the development of real observational skills.

Finally, ask the children to draw their own self-portraits. Ask them to take enormous care to check every detail in the mirrors and remind them that there should be more looking than drawing!

Further activities
• If the children have drawn each other, display these portraits alongside the respective self-portraits and encourage the children to compare the results.
• Repeat the activity using a range of curved reflective surfaces such as spoons (an inverted image!), shiny utensils, smoothed tinfoil or convex/concave/rippled mirrors. These results can be amazing and form an excellent link with science.
• Repeat the activity using pastels on very dark paper.

18 | Chapter 1

9. String patterns

Objective
To develop an awareness of line and pattern by 'drawing' with threads.

Age range
Seven to eleven.

Group size
Whole class or groups.

Time
At least 45 minutes.

What you need
A piece of card (20cm × 10cm) for each child, string and other threads of various thicknesses (preferably white or all one colour), PVA adhesive, spreaders, scissors.

What you do
Give each child a piece of card and explain that they are going to draw using threads, making patterns which will cover the whole card until no background is showing through. Demonstrate how they can coat portions of the card with the adhesive and then cut a length of thread to stick down on the card. Talk about the way the threads can be arranged. Encourage the children to use words such as curled, coiled, wavy, spiked, jagged, striped and so on. Write the words down where the children can see them to act as a reminder. Now ask the children to use as many different threads as they can, arranged in as many ways as possible, to cover all the card. As the cards are completed, arrange them in a chequer-board pattern. This should form an exciting reference and display, enabling children to see a very wide range of line patterns.

Further activities
• Photocopy the cards and mount the results together to show the tonal effects of the line patterns.
• Photocopy each child's pattern and then let them cut the copies into squares. Ask them to rearrange the pieces, sticking them down to make even more elaborate line patterns.
• Use the results as patterns for embroidery and/or collage.

Drawing and mark-making 19

10. Black and white

Objective
To look at pattern work in drawing for illustration.

Age range
Nine to eleven.

Group size
Whole class or small groups.

Time
One hour.

What you need
A4 white paper, A4 black paper, black ink and pens or black felt-tipped pens, white paint, thin brushes, examples of William Morris book illustration, for example, *The Kelmscott Chaucer*, or copies of photocopiable page 171.

What to do
Show the children examples of the black and white ornamentation sometimes used for text illustration in printing and distribute copies of photocopiable page 171 which gives an appropriate example. Explain that designers such as William Morris would plan and draw out the patterns using black inks and would work at their patterns, using white paint to go over any sections they wanted to correct, until they were satisfied with the results. (This could be used to form links with work in history on the Victorians.)

Working first on the white paper, ask the children to draw a frame around the edge of the sheets, leaving a space in the middle for an illustration or for a piece of their own work to be mounted. Next ask them to use the black inks to draw a suitable pattern to decorate the frame. If they want to correct a line in the wrong place, show them how to block it out with white pigment, working in the same way as the Victorian illustrative designers! If a particular piece of work is to be displayed within the frame, perhaps a poem or story, encourage the children to try to make the pattern reflect the same theme (for example, animals, characters and so on).

When these initial designs are completed, ask the children to work with the black paper and white paints to produce the same pattern but in reverse – forming a negative image.

The two images should be displayed together and compared.

Further activities
• Let the children enlarge small sections of their patterns.
• Use the same techniques to illustrate books written by the children, letters home to parents, school presentation certificates, bookplates, invitations and so on.
• Encourage the children to compare the illustration with medieval manuscripts such as the Book of Kells. This could be linked with a study of other times and cultures.

11. Negative spaces

Objective
To encourage careful observation.

Age range
Seven to eleven.

Group size
Small groups.

Time
At least 30 minutes.

What you need
An arrangement of artefacts (for example, cogs, wheels, tins, utensils, books, equipment, cups and mugs, toys and so on), paper, a range of drawing tools.

What to do
Ask the children to sit in a group around the still life display so that each has a different viewpoint. Ask the children to look carefully at the objects, particularly at the spaces between them. You will need to point some of these out. Tell the children that these are called 'negative spaces'.

Now ask the children to draw only the shapes of the spaces not the actual objects themselves. Explain that the artefacts will emerge as if by magic if the spaces between them are drawn well! Initially this can be tricky for children, so be sure to circulate among them as they begin to work. Point out the spaces from each viewpoint and encourage lots of careful looking.

Next ask the children to block in the spaces as thickly and darkly as possible. This will give the effect of negative images which can be extremely dramatic. Once this is done, let them add more details to the exposed outlines of the objects. It can be effective to let the children select only one or two artefacts to be worked on in this way, leaving the others as white areas.

This activity is designed to help children use a wider range of reference points when they are drawing than merely the outlines of things – and it encourages much more careful looking and, therefore, better quality observational drawings.

Drawing and mark-making

12. Sketch books

Objective
To establish the habit of using a sketch book regularly and to build up a bank of working drawings.

Age range
Seven to eleven.

Group size
Whole class, groups and individuals.

Time
Ongoing work.

What you need
A sketch book for each child, a range of drawing pencils, specimen sketch books and copies of artists' working drawings.

What to do
Show the children some examples of real sketch books. (You could ask your local secondary schools or colleges if they could help with the loan of some.) If possible, show children working drawings taken from illustrations of a range of artists' work.

Explain that a sketch book is a visual record of observations and ideas, with a collection of shapes, patterns and notes which can be used later for incorporating into more detailed work.

Give each child a sketch book and some drawing pencils. Ask the children to draw on the first page something which is in the classroom only temporarily. This could be flowers, a plant, some artefacts linked to a display or, equipment on loan etc. Ask them to record the object in their sketches as it is now. Talk about the way in which things change over time, for example growth, change of seasons, altering furnishings and decorations at home, fashion and so on.

Set aside a time each week for children to add to their sketch books. You could incorporate a tour around the school grounds into the activity. This would supply the children with a rich source of material to draw. Explain that children can write notes and add words to their drawings to make a fuller record. Ask them always to write the date, place and time by their sketches (Figure 1).

Get in the habit of always letting the children use their sketch books on school visits or when planning designs. Ask them to look through these books *before* starting any painting, craft work or illustration to search for ideas, patterns and drawings to develop.

Regularly ask the children to share their books with each other, talking about why they chose to draw and record objects in the way they did. This forms excellent links with English work.

Set up 'mini-exhibitions' of the sketch books for other children and visitors to see. Just as you would regularly check the children's exercise books, spend a little time reviewing each child's sketch book and discussing their ideas. It is essential that the children realise that this work is valued and needs to be of quality.

When full, these sketch books should be kept by the children for future reference. A good place to keep them is in the class library area. They are a valuable reference source not just for art but also for history, geography, mathematics and English – particularly poetry and creative writing.

Figure 1

CHAPTER 2

Painting

Just like drawing, there's no right or wrong way to paint. The exciting thing about painting is the freshness and vitality that children achieve by experimenting freely with images, textures and colour. However, children do need to explore some of the formal elements of painting in order to understand the basic principles of mixing and the use of colour to convey different moods and ideas, times and seasons (for example, Monet's Rouen Cathedral and Haystacks).

The children also need to experience using a range of different types of paint and investigate the effects that can be obtained by using many kinds of brushes or painting tools.

Primary children should have access to powder paint, ready-mixed paints, tempera, watercolours, poster paint, gouache and acrylics. There should be a good selection of brushes and tools to choose from, including round- and straight-ended bristle brushes, soft 'watercolour' brushes, large and small brushes, palette knives, spreaders and sponges, plus home-made experimental painting tools, for example, rags wound on sticks. Mixing palettes are also needed but a good cheap alternative can be old plates – particularly the plastic type once used for school meals!

BACKGROUND

As children progress through school, they should have increased opportunities to experience different media and experiment with techniques so that they are able to build up a growing bank of possible choices to help them express their ideas through painting. They should also have the chance to explore the properties of different papers and surfaces to work on and to learn how paint reacts when applied to them.

Activities should be organised to enable children to work at different scales – from delicate small illustrations to really large paintings – and to work both independently and on group projects. Don't forget that painting can be developed into three dimensions!

ACTIVITIES

1. Fading colour squares

Objective
To develop children's appreciation of the subtleties of colour.

Age range
Seven to eleven.

Group size
Whole class or groups.

Time
45 minutes.

What you need
A large sheet of paper for each child, mixing palettes, brushes and water pots, powder paint (black, white and one other colour).

What to do
Show the children how to fold the sheet to form 16 rectangles as in Figure 1. (This forms useful links with maths.)

Ask the children to use the poster paints to mix the darkest colour they can to paint the first square. Then ask them to mix a slightly lighter colour and paint in the second square. Let the children repeat the process until the whole grid is painted with becoming (Figure 2). This can useful links with Science.

This is more difficult than it might appear. When the paint is dry, ask the children to invent names for their colour squares, for example, midnight forest green, foggy red, frostsparkle. This can be used as an excellent link with language development.

Further activity
Older children who are learning to use pairs of compasses and protractors could be asked to construct a colour shade wheel by dividing a circle into 12 sections.

Figure 1

Figure 2

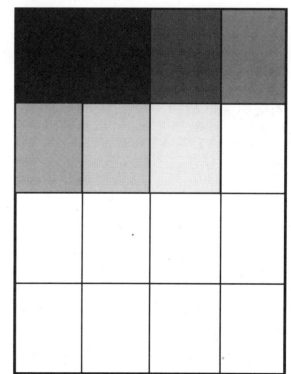

Painting 25

2. Natural colour match

Objective
To extend children's awareness of colour in the natural world.

Age range
Seven to eleven.

Time
30 minutes.

What you need
Colour grids (see previous activity) in green, brown, yellow and red.

What to do
Take the children out into the school grounds with their colour grids. Ask them to find leaves, stones, flowers, bark and other natural materials which match any of the colour squares.

If possible, bring samples of these back into the classroom to display and classify as 'natural materials'. Ask the children to bring in from home manufactured items to match in the same way, for example, wool, fabric, crayons, papers and so on. Ask them to classify these into 'natural' and 'manufactured' categories.

3. Camouflage

Objective
To develop colour matching and painting skills.

Age range
Nine to eleven.

Group size
Whole class or smaller groups.

What you need
Photographs of animals which use camouflage, a selection of small scraps of patterned fabric about 10cm squared, paper, powder paints, brushes, palettes, water pots and paper adhesive.

What to do
Talk to the children about camouflage and its function and show them some examples of animal camouflage. Talk about how people have developed camouflage, for example, to prevent soldiers, battleships and planes being observed. This could be used to form links with history. Look at the fabrics and discuss their colours, patterns and texture. Ask the children to stick the scrap of material somewhere on a sheet of paper. Then ask them to use paint and to match the colours and pattern on the paper around it, until it is hard to see the separate fabric. Emphasise the fact that they really have to look carefully to do this.

This can also be done as a group activity with two or three children working together.

Further activities
• Repeat the exercise using animal pictures instead of fabric.
• Link the work with analysis of different materials, for example, cotton, foil and plastic.

26 Chapter 2

4. Impasto

Objective
To give children experience of working with very thick paint and paint spreaders; to consider the work of an artist who worked in this way.

Age range
Seven to eleven.

Group size
Whole class or groups.

Time
One hour.

What you need
Some prints of Van Gogh's paintings, powder paints mixed very thickly with PVA medium adhesive (or acrylic paints), palette knives or spreaders or flat lolly sticks, mixing palettes or plates, cardboard or hardboard offcuts, photocopier.

What to do
Begin by talking about artists who use very thick paint. Show the children the Van Gogh prints and explain that prints cannot show how thickly the paint is laid down. Explain also that artists sometimes use palette knives to achieve special effects with thick or scraped paint.

Explain that the children are to paint a picture using a similar technique and suggest that they paint a similar subject to the examples you have used initially, for example, flowers, their bedroom or a chair, so that their ideas can be compared with Van Gogh's impressions.

Ask the children to paint thickly on to the card, using the palette knives or spreaders to mix the paint and lay it down boldly on the surface. When the paintings are completed and dry – acrylic paint will dry very quickly – display them around the room. Let the children walk around the 'exhibition'. Encourage them to look particularly at the way the paint has been laid on the card and at the marks made by the spreaders. Discuss any interesting effects that have been achieved where the colours have merged or have been scraped together.

Now let them look again at the Van Gogh prints and consider the same points on these pictures.

Photocopy some of the children's work to show how their paintings would look as black and white prints.

Painting 27

5. Restricted palette painting

Objective
To develop the use of tone in painting.

Age range
Five to eleven.

Group size
Small groups or whole class.

Time
One hour.

What you need
Paper, brushes, palettes, water pots, mirrors, powder colour or tempera blocks in black, white and one colour, examples of artists' work using restricted colours.

What to do
Refer to the activity 'On your marks – 1' on page 11 and discuss the idea of tone. Ask the children to half close their eyes and look at an object, noticing how the darkest areas seem to stand out and the lighter ones recede.

Next ask the children to paint something that they can observe at first hand, for example, an artefact or a building. Explain that they can only use the restricted colours. Younger children can be asked to observe their own faces using mirrors, then paint a self-portrait using the restricted colours. Alternatively, they can be asked to paint a portrait of a classmate. Show the children examples of portraits painted in restricted colours, for example, Henri Matisse's *The Green Line – Portrait of Madame Matisse*.

Further activities
- Develop the idea further by showing examples of other artists' work such as Picasso's blue period paintings.
- Restrict different groups of children to using particular colours and then compare the green group with the red, blue, yellow and so on.
- Photocopy the children's paintings to illustrate the tonal quality (which is very apparent in this black and white form).

6. Colour washes

Objective
To investigate the properties of watercolour paints and to introduce the idea of covering large areas of paper.

Age range
Seven to eleven.

Group size
Small groups.

Time
At least 30 minutes.

What you need
Large soft brushes, watercolour or tempera paints, palettes, water pots, A4 sheets of heavy quality paper, boards or easels.

What to do
Ask the children to fasten the paper to a board or easel so that water can gently roll down when brushed on to the sheet. Demonstrate how to load a brush heavily with water and sweep it horizontally across the top of the paper. Repeat this twice.

Mix some coloured paint and, keeping it very wet, brush it across the wet topmost section of the paper, letting it run down the sheet. Reload the brush and sweep this across the next section of paper, again letting the colour run down the sheet. Work fairly swiftly repeating this process until all the sheet is covered. Draw the children's attention to the effects obtained.

Now let the children experiment with the same process, working in a variety of colours.

Further activities
• Use the sheets as backgrounds for poetry, descriptive writing or written work describing the colour wash process.
• Tear up the strips from different sheets to make into paper weaving.
• Use the sheets to make book jackets.
• Save the completed sheets to act as backgrounds for the following activity or other art work.

Painting 29

7. 'Framed' plants

Objective
To concentrate on small detailed work.

Age range
Five to eleven.

Group size
Small groups.

Time
At least one hour.

What you need
A frame of paper or card 10cm × 15cm (see 'Viewfinders', page 15), paper, watercolour paints, soft brushes, palettes and water pots, A4 or A5 sheets of paper, pencils, a vase containing a leaf, plant or flower.

What to do
Before undertaking this activity, it would be helpful if children had already experienced Activity 6. They can then use the colour washes to form a background for this work. Ask the children to experiment with the paints and see what colours they can achieve. Encourage them to experiment by using differing amounts of water on the brush. Talk about the effects that can be achieved and in particular the transparency and delicacy of the colours when more water is used.

Ask the children to sit in a group around a plant or flower in a vase, so they all have a different view. Give the children the viewfinder frames and ask them to move the frames around and look through them until they find part of the object that particularly appeals to them, for example, part of a leaf.

Ask the children to sketch the outline of their chosen view very lightly on to the paper. Make sure not to let this part of the process become more than establishing a guideline – the concentration should be on the painting. Explain that in watercolour painting the technique is to paint the palest areas first, adding the darkest sections later. Ask the children to work with care to paint the 'framed' section and to concentrate only on those details within the frame. Because the children will choose different sections and different views, the group will produce an excellent visual record of the plant or flowers.

This activity is particularly useful for recording life cycles and growth of plants or close observation and recording of artefacts linked to topic work.

30 Chapter 2

8. Graphical painting

Objective
To develop the work on mark-making (see Chapter One), with the addition of selecting colour and pattern; to consider the work of pop artists (for example, Andy Warhol – famous for his Soup Cans etc; Jasper Johns – utilising numbers and letters in his work).

Age range
Seven to eleven.

Group size
Whole class working in pairs.

Time
At least one hour.

What you need
Children's drawings based on lettering (see, for example, 'Names' on page 82), a frame of card or paper 10cm × 5cm, A3 paper, paints, different sized brushes, palettes, water pots, pencils, examples of work by pop artists such as Andy Warhol, Jasper Johns, Roy Lichtenstein, Robert Indiana and Joe Tilson.

What to do
Ask the children to work in pairs to discuss their drawings and then to choose which of their lettering designs they wish to develop. Show the children examples of the work of pop artists who have used lettering in their work and discuss the ways in which the artists have chosen to paint using areas of flat colour. Let the children take their card frames and move them around their designs until they find an interesting area which appeals to them. Ask them to draw very lightly around the inside edge of the frame to mark their chosen section.

Next demonstrate how to 'square up' these sections (see page 15). Ask the children to transfer the grid on to an A3 sheet of paper. (You can extend the mathematics by asking the children to say how much larger the new design will be!)

If this is too difficult for the children, ask them just to divide the drawing into halves, quarters, eighths and sixteenths. Next, ask them to divide the A3 sheet into a matching number of rectangles by simple folding.

Check that the grids are drawn properly. Then ask the children to look carefully at each square and to draw an enlarged version on the new sheet. Ask them either to match their original choice of colour (warm or cold) or to change it and to paint their designs.

When the children have been working for some time, stop them and ask them to talk about their paintings and any problems they have experienced – and how they have solved them. Encourage them to discuss each other's work in a positive manner.
• Can you tell me something that you like about this design?
• Why do you think this choice of colour is interesting?

When the work is completed, it should be mounted alongside the original design so that it is clear how the development has been made.

Painting 31

9. Supplement extensions

Objective
To enable children to look at subtle colour changes and replicate them.

Age range
Seven to eleven.

Group size
Small groups or whole class.

Time
One hour.

What you need
A selection of colour pictures cut from magazines, scissors, a range of coloured pencils or pastels, sheets of paper (as large as the cuttings), paper adhesive.

What to do
Distribute the pictures to the children and ask them to cut them into two pieces. Ask them to stick one piece of the picture on to a sheet of paper, leaving sufficient space to complete the missing section of the picture.

Let the children complete the missing half of the drawing, first drawing in the outline and then colouring it in, carefully matching the colours as exactly as possible, constantly referring to the other part of the picture.

This is a useful exercise to link in with a project theme by selecting suitable illustrations to match the topic, for example, animals, portraits, homes and so on.

Further activities
• The same idea can be used with photographs – even better if the children have taken them personally – postcards, posters and old books too 'tatty' for further library use.
• For older children the activity can be further extended by only giving them one section of the cutting and letting them use their imagination to complete the whole picture. If you give the other half to another child it is most interesting to compare the results, but make sure they do not see each other's interpretation until they have finished!

32 Chapter 2

10. Mega-matching

Objective
To develop colour matching skills and enlargement ideas.

Age range
Nine to eleven.

Group size
Whole class or small groups.

Time
One hour.

What you need
An illustration of an interesting painting, scissors, adhesive, ruler, a selection of coloured pencils, pastels or paints, small brushes, palettes, water pots, sheets of A4 paper.

What to do
Mount the picture on to card and cut it up into rectangles of approximately 4cm × 3cm. Number the rectangles consecutively on the back.

Tell the children that you are going to give them a mystery to solve. Explain that you are going to give them each a clue and that they must match colours carefully to produce a giant copy of the picture that has been cut up.

Give each child a section of the illustration and a sheet of A4 paper. Ask them to look carefully at their cards and talk about the colours and shapes they see. Ask them to look particularly at the edges of the card and to make a note of where any lines or colours come. Show the children how to transfer the colours and lines printed on their pieces of card by drawing them on to the equivalent place on the A4 sheet. Introduce the idea of estimation:
• How far along the side does the blue mark come on this card?
• Where does it go next?
• Does it go straight down or at an angle?

Demonstrate how to fill in rough guidelines in pencil for shapes and colour blocks. Next ask the children to reproduce their cards, enlarging them on to the paper, matching the colours and shapes as closely as possible. Explain that they must take great care so that the mystery can be solved! When the children have finished, ask them to write on the back of their paper the same number that is on the back of their clue. Then using the numbers for reference, start assembling the huge picture asking the children to match their sections together using colour and adjoining shapes as a guide. Encourage plenty of discussion about the matching process!

The results are usually amazing – and it gives you an instant wall of display of massive proportions!

Painting   33

11. Wet pebbles

Objective
To develop close observational skills.

Age range
Nine to eleven.

Group size
Small groups.

Time
30 minutes.

What you need
A collection of interesting shaped pebbles, a bowl of water, hand-held magnifying lenses, watercolour paints, palettes, water pots, a range of watercolour brushes, good quality cartridge paper, scrap paper, examples of watercolour paintings.

What to do
Put the pebbles in a bowl of water, then let each child take a wet pebble from the bowl and examine it carefully using the magnifying lenses. Ask them to describe the shape and surface texture, whether it is smooth or pitted, cracked or sharp etc. Write down the words they use to describe the pebbles. (These can be used later alongside the paintings to extend English work.) Go on to discuss the colours, noting particularly how the colours may change across the surface or be different inside cracks or crevices. If the stones dry out in the children's hands, let them re-wet them, noting how the wetness brings out more colour.

Now let the children experiment with their watercolour paints. Demonstrate how to charge a brush with water and pick up just a little amount of pigment from the colour tray then swirl it on to a piece of scrap paper. Ask the group to use brushes of different sizes and see what effects they can achieve with loose brushstrokes in different colours. Let them investigate what happens when they use more pigment, or drop different colours on to already wet surfaces. Stop the activity when everyone has had a chance to try a variety of techniques. Now ask each child in turn to explain how they made the different paint patterns and which ones would be the most useful in painting their chosen pebble. Spend a few minutes comparing the swirls and looking at each child's stone, discussing any suitable 'matches' of effect.

Now let the children paint a large watercolour picture of their pebble, without any initial drawing. Encourage them to work by blocking in light areas of colour first, then gradually adding darker shades and detail over the top. Point out that watercolour artists always work from light tones to dark tones, adding fine detail last.

If possible, try to show the children some examples of watercolour paintings or book illustrations. Edith Holden's *The Country Diary of an Edwardian Lady* might be a useful resource for closely observed nature watercolours.

CHAPTER 3

Printmaking

Children can gain immense pleasure and acquire a vast range of skills through printmaking in school. There is a real sense of magic when a child reveals her first print because the image is, of course, reversed and the initial drawing or arrangement can truly be looked at as if with fresh eyes. Do not miss the chance to watch the children's faces as they peel back their paper and glimpse their prints; you will be rewarded! There are wonderful opportunities for language development here, such as the introduction of terms such as 'reversal', 'negative image' and 'pattern'.

Printmaking can be very easy or very complex. A print can be used for just one edition or for multiple purposes, producing patterns and designs as the basis for other artwork where other media are used over the prints. For instance, a simple drawing on a polystyrene printing tile might be re-inked and printed about 20 times to make a repeat pattern. On the other hand, a Formica table-top print might be the sole print produced.

Children can learn the basic idea of printmaking simply through the early activities in this section and then go on to look at simple screen printing.

Printmaking 35

BACKGROUND

Printmaking can be developed in numerous ways and it is possible to allow continuity throughout the school with printmaking forming part of an art programme for all ages. An example of this might be where a child makes a print on paper in only one colour, then cuts away part of the first printing 'block' and re-inks it in another colour, adding to the original image and producing a multi-coloured print. That child could then go on to print on to different materials and fabrics and then work on top of these with other media, using perhaps inks, pastels, paints or threads to develop their ideas further. It is fascinating to see the wide range of work which can be developed from a common starting point.

Printmaking can enrich any topic work very effectively and extend children's learning. For example, simple prints, based on detailed drawings of artefacts used in history studies, can encourage children to make and record really accurate observations. This process could also be used with science work – for example in recording plant growth, showing weather changes and effects or illustrating electrical circuits. Similarly in geography simple maps, plans and trails could be printed out (taking care over the reversal effects!) or a study of pattern-making in different cultures could be recorded through printmaking. Mathematical skills need to be used if children are to investigate accurate layouts for repeated or dropped repeat pattern making (Figure 1), with careful measuring of the printing area and careful estimation of relative positions when the print is placed on the paper or fabric.

Costumes for drama or other special productions in school can be made using printing skills to make beautifully patterned and coloured items out of otherwise dull fabrics or tired dressing-up clothes. Children can also print on relatively cheap fabrics to make their own curtains for puppet theatres, home-play areas, book corners or even the library. In the same way, they can produce cushions or table

Figure 1

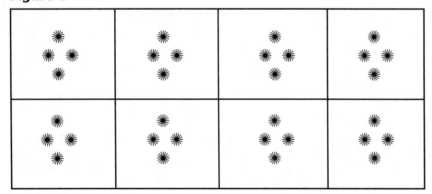

Repeat pattern

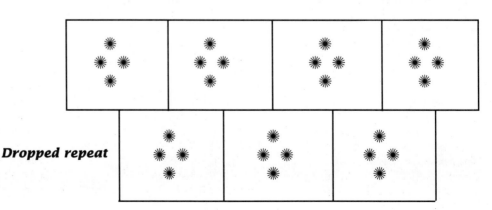

Dropped repeat

coverings to enhance the school environment both aesthetically and functionally.

The range of equipment needed for printmaking is fairly cost-effective. Many of the items needed, such as rollers and squeegees (ink spreaders), can be bought and, if kept carefully, will last for years and years. Other items will need replenishing of course, but in general they are not wildly expensive. Water-based printing inks, for example, can be used sparingly and therefore last well. Materials for printing blocks can often be made from scrap materials, although packs of polystyrene printing tiles – obtainable through educational suppliers – are an excellent investment as they can be used successfully with all ages, even very young children. They can be used simply or in highly sophisticated ways. Although these tiles come in a fairly large size they are easily cut down to a smaller, more manageable size.

Many materials can be obtained virtually free of charge, for example, packing cases, string and card.

Initially at least, it is a good idea to let children work with small sections until they understand the printing process fully and are more confident. The blocks are fairly robust and will normally give about 20 good prints before the surface begins to deteriorate. (Even if there appears to be a chance of reusing an old tile this is unadvisable as the results are rarely satisfactory. It is better to use a fresh tile for every new design.) Polystyrene printing tiles are easy to clean under a tap and can be displayed alongside the finished prints.

A suggested equipment list for each class or year group would be:
• six rollers in different widths for dry rollering;
• six rollers in different widths for ink rollering;
• a selection of water-based printing inks stored in a tray;
• six boards for the ink rollering (Formica offcuts are useful. Plate glass is excellent but must be used with care);
• a box of polystyrene printing tiles.

These items can be stored in a central place and, if funds are tight, shared between more than one class. It is important to teach children to take great care of the equipment. This

Printmaking

can be made easier by always storing the printing rollers and inks together – a plastic box or 'cleaning materials' storage tray with a handle can be useful here. Another useful tip is to mark the handles of the dry rollers in some distinctive way, with paint or coloured tape for instance. This will help remind the children to use them only for clean work.

Another invaluable help would be the designation of a print drying area. Prints can be left to dry flat if space allows but otherwise rig up a length of strong string across a suitable corner of the room and use clothes pegs to fasten wet prints to the line – safely out of harm's way!

It would also be useful to try to find some examples of artists' work as printmakers. There are many examples by Andy Warhol but don't forget examples of printed materials such as wallpapers (and the work of William Morris and John Dearle), poster designers (Toulouse-Lautrec, Alphonse Mucha) and the exquisite Japanese prints of Hokusai. Do not worry if you do not have a detailed knowledge of the work of printmakers – you can always show the children how to use reference materials or contact local galleries and find out together! Many galleries and bookshops sell collections of wallpaper and fabric designs from different periods and cultures and these are generally very useful, being both reasonably priced and full of sheets which can be pulled out and displayed to good effect.

Do not forget either that there are a lot of examples to be found very near to home – think of local posters, book illustrations, gift wrapping papers, paper and plastic bags, wallpapers and decorative papers. The children could make a collection of printed materials and use this as an interesting starting point for their investigations into printmaking. You may even have a local printer or newspaper publisher who would be pleased to talk to the children or host a class visit to their workplace, making a very useful link with industry with scope for cross-curricular elements.

ACTIVITIES

1. Formica monoprinting

Objective
To introduce the idea of printing.

Age range
Five to eleven.

Group size
Small groups or pairs.

Time
20 minutes.

What you need
A4 paper, offcuts of Formica (or table-top!), rollers, water-based printing ink, range of drawing tools (sticks, brush ends, ballpoint pens, pencils etc).

What to do
Squeeze a small amount of printing ink on to the Formica, then use a roller to spread this evenly but thinly (be careful, too much ink will spoil the result).

Show the children how to lower the paper carefully on to the Formica. Explain that they should not touch the paper with anything other than the drawing tool – all impressions will show up on the print! Encourage them to draw a design heavily on the paper, then gently peel the paper from the Formica and reveal the design in colour on the reverse. Be careful not to disturb the design on the Formica.

Next, show them how to put a fresh piece of paper carefully over the ink and use a dry roller to roll firmly over the surface of the paper. Once more peel back the paper – a negative of the design will be revealed!

A tiny extra amount of ink will now be needed and should be rolled out again with the ink roller, ready for the next piece of work.

Be careful – over-inking will result in a smudged design and a disappointed pupil.

Further activities
• Ink up the Formica as before. Tear up scraps of paper (or make small paper shapes) and arrange them randomly on the ink. Cover the Formica with a sheet of paper and dry roller the paper. Peel off as before.
• Tear up scraps of paper and print as above then draw linking lines between the paper shapes and experiment with different patterns and designs.

Printmaking

2. Sponge prints

Objective
To experiment with printmaking.

Age range
Five to eleven.

Group size
Small groups.

Time
30 minutes.

What you need
Paper (A3 or larger), water-based printing inks (in shallow dishes or saucers), offcuts or shapes in foam sponge or small natural sponges.

What to do
Put small amounts of printing inks into saucers or similar, then let the children choose a sponge shape and dip it into one colour. Ask them to press the sponge on to their paper, to make a print. This can be randomly or in lines or patterns – let the children experiment.

When the print is dry, let the children use a second colour with a different sponge shape. Alternatively, let them put the second colour on while the first layer is still wet and experiment with different effects where the colours blend.

Further activities
• Pre-mix lighter and darker shades of the same colours (by adding black or white to the base colour) and limit the colour palette.
• Let the children print on a variety of different coloured papers, or different textured papers (eg. rough, smooth, different wallpapers, greaseproof). Encourage the children to look at and discuss different absorbencies and effects.
• Let the children print using basic colour then pass the print on to another pupil to add second or third prints in rotation using a contrasting colour.
• Use the printed sheets as mounts for other prints.
• Substitute crumpled newspaper for sponges for a different effect.

3. Screen printing

Objective
To introduce simple screen printing techniques.

Age range
Nine to eleven.

Group size
Small groups.

Time
At least 45 minutes.

What you need
Designs from previous activities, coloured sugar paper, A3 cartridge paper, a squeegee (to fit screen), a wooden frame (the screen – this can be made from any framing or standard 2" × 1" wooden battens), staple gun and staples, mesh materials, (curtain mesh, nylon etc), plant spray, water-based screen printing inks, scissors, brown parcel tape.

What to do
Ask at least two children to work together to stretch the mesh tightly over the wooden frame and secure it firmly by stapling it to the sides of the frame. Explain that a taut finish is essential and that they can achieve a tighter

40 Chapter 3

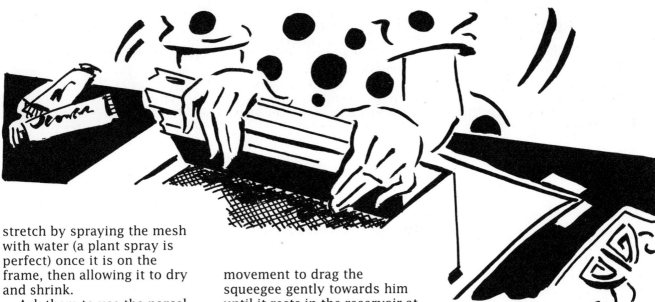

stretch by spraying the mesh with water (a plant spray is perfect) once it is on the frame, then allowing it to dry and shrink.

Ask them to use the parcel tape on the inside of the frame to seal the gap between the mesh and the frame. Show them how to fasten an extra width (about 5cm) of tape at either end of the screen to act as a reservoir for the inks.

Next let the children choose a design and prepare a stencil by cutting away those sections they want to print. Explain that they must be careful not to have the remaining areas too flimsy – bold designs are best to begin with. As they gain confidence, they can experiment with more complex and subtle designs.

Prepare a small pile of cartridge paper on which to print as they will need this soft base to achieve a better contact with the mesh. Show the group how to place the stencil on top of the first printing sheet, then set the screen carefully on top of that. Demonstrate how to run a strip of screen printing ink across the reservoir they have created inside the screen. Ask one of the children to hold the screen firmly, then let another put the squeegee into the reservoir behind the ink and use firm pressure and a slow movement to drag the squeegee gently towards him until it rests in the reservoir at his end of the screen. Encourage the child to hold the squeegee in place to retain the remaining ink and carefully raise the screen – not too high – from the print. The stencil will be stuck to the underside of the mesh. Ask a child to remove the print from the wadge and leave it to dry.

Ask the child holding the screen to lower it back in place and hold it firmly while another child drags the squeegee firmly back towards her – thus creating another print. Depending on the quality of the stencil, the children will be able to create a number of successful prints. Encourage them to experiment with different papers. Explain that the fundamental principle of screen printing is that a number of repeat prints can be made.

At the end of the session, make sure the children wash the mesh thoroughly in a large sink or gently hose it down outside over a drain. The mesh can then be re-used.

Further activities
• Overprint in a different colour on a previous dry print but printing slightly off-centre of the original (working from dark colours to light colours).
• Cut a new stencil and overprint.
• Cut random shapes of paper (or mathematical shapes or themed shapes, such as animals) and print.
• Use more than one colour of ink in the reservoir, but do not mix them – let the squeegee action do this for you. Some wonderful effects can be achieved.
• Print first without a stencil to prepare a background. When the paper is dry, print a design on top.
• The same technique can be used on textiles, but a long table with a soft bed of old blankets etc, taped firmly down and covered with polythene is needed. Stretch the fabric taut over the printing table and secure it. Then stretch cotton threads across to mark sections for repeat patterns. Lift the screen along the fabric to repeat the prints. Check first that your inks are suitable for fabric printing.

4. Shoe box screen printing

Objective
To experience screen printing with everyday materials.

Age range
Seven to eleven.

Time
At least one hour.

Group size
Small groups.

What you need
A suitable design (see previous activities), sturdy shoe box, scissors, mesh material (curtain mesh, nylon etc.), brown parcel tape, PVA adhesive, water-based screen printing inks, coloured sugar paper, cartridge paper.

What to do
Help the children cut out the base of the shoe box, leaving a 5cm flange around the edge, then ask them to cut out a piece of mesh large enough to fit the whole base. Get them to spread adhesive on the cardboard flange and stretch the mesh over the cut-out sticking it firmly to the cardboard edges. Leave the adhesive to dry. When it is quite dry, ask the group to use the parcel tape to ensure that the mesh is absolutely secure. Explain that they should make sure the tape goes slightly up the sides of the box to protect the cardboard from the inks. Show them how to run an extra thickness of tape at both ends of the mesh to form reservoirs for the inks.

The squeegee, or spreader, now needs to be made from the lid of the box – or another piece of stout cardboard. Ensure that the children cut the cardboard squeegee so that it fits comfortably in the width of the box.

Now let the group choose a design and prepare a stencil by cutting away those sections they want to print, then let them print as in the previous activity.

Further activities
- Print on to a range of different papers (colour, weight, etc. for example tracing paper).
- The same method can be used on textiles and T-shirts but fabric inks must be used. When printing on T-shirts, remember to insert a pad of paper between the printed front and the back!
- Banners and flags (for example school crest for fêtes, open days and sports days) can be printed.

5. String patterns

Objective
To explore printmaking using simple blocks.

Age range
Five to eleven.

Group size
Small groups.

Time
One hour (over two sessions).

What you need
Paper, pencils, viewfinder (optional), small wooden offcuts or pieces of cardboard, string, scissors, PVA adhesive, paper to print on, water-based printing ink, rollers, printing trays (to contain inks), adhesive tape.

What to do
Ask the children to produce a design based on line (see Chapter One, 'Drawing and mark-making') and choose a section with interesting patterns. (Using a viewfinder would help.) Get them to draw this chosen design on to the wood or card, then cut lengths of string and stick the pieces along the design. Leave it to dry.

Show the children how to put a small amount of ink into the printing tray and spread it with the roller until it is evenly covered. Let them each roll the ink on to their prepared string blocks. When the string is coated with the ink, show them how to pick the block up carefully and lower it ink side down on to the printing paper. Explain that to ensure a good print they should roll a dry roller several times on the clean side of the block. Then let them lift the blocks and repeat the printing process as required. It should be possible to use each block to make many satisfactory prints. Leave the prints to dry.

Further activities
• Overprint (on dry prints) in lighter colours.
• Print closely together to make a line or a block repeat.
• Print with a half-drop (Figure 1) to make a more exciting pattern.
• Make up a wooden block and use fabric printing inks to print on to textiles. This is more satisfactory if you fasten a handle (for example, a piece of card or a clothes peg held in place with adhesive, nails etc) on to the back of the block. Make a wad (about 15cm × 10cm) of soft absorbent fabric. Saturate this with thick fabric ink and use it as a stamping pad to ink up the printing block. Hold the block by the handle and rock it from side to side to ensure good inking. Then print as described in the activity.
• Use string prints to overprint earlier screen prints.
• When the prints are finished, display the blocks alongside the designs.
• Produce string patterns in letter, word, number or mathematical shapes to reinforce other curriculum areas.
• Impress the finished blocks into soft clay to make tile patterns (see Chapter Four, 'Ceramics').
• Instead of making string blocks, print with small wooden offcuts which can be scored or have pieces of cardboard stuck on them. Use them to print on top of earlier string prints.
• Make photocopies of the string blocks – the effects are amazing! Build a whole panel of these photocopies.

6. Press print pictures

Objective
To explore repeat patterns in printmaking.

Age range
Five to eleven.

Group size
Whole class or small group. (If the whole class prepare their prints together it will be necessary to take turns in printing.)

Time
One hour.

What you need
Polystyrene printing tiles, pencils, children's own drawings/designs, dry rollers, ink rollers, Formica offcuts (20cm × 30cm), A2 sheets of paper, scissors and craft knives, paper towels, examples of a repeat pattern (on wallpaper etc.), tracing paper.

What to do
Explain that the children are going to make their own prints with a repeat pattern. Show them an example of a print where the pattern has been repeated in some way. Ask them to think how this has been done. Has the pattern been repeated side by side? Is it directly underneath? Is it underneath but moved slightly to one side? (This is called a half-drop repeat pattern.) Is it reversed and turned upside down? Ask the children to think of as many ways as possible that a pattern could be repeated. Give out polystyrene printing tiles cut to a size you feel is appropriate. If the children are experienced and have sufficient skills to produce highly detailed work and are confident in working 'large', you may wish to give them full or half sheets, but for early work quarter-sized sections are recommended.

Now ask the children to take their own drawings and designs and look at them carefully. Tell the children that they can draw their designs on to the polystyrene using ordinary pencils and pressing fairly hard. Talk about the fact that anything they draw will be reversed when it is printed and ask them to remember that any words or numbers will have to be drawn in reverse in order to be printed correctly. If anyone wishes to use words or numbers, let them write their design on tracing paper first, then turn it over to see how they will need to draw on their tile.

Point out that tiny details will be lost in the printing process so it is better for them to make clear line drawings. However, encourage them to experiment with using dots, crossed lines and other marks to make their design interesting. Check that the children are drawing their lines heavily enough to make a clear indent but not so heavily that it cuts the tile right through! (If there is an accident, however, the tile can be taped together on the back with adhesive tape.)

Demonstrate to one group at a time how to make the print by squeezing a little blob (about the size of a grape) of one of the lighter coloured water-based printing inks on to the Formica offcut. Make sure that the children understand that you are going to use an inking roller for the next part of the process. Using the roller, first spread the ink widely over the Formica and then roll it out to spread the ink thinly and to coat the roller evenly. Then place the polystyrene tile on to a sheet of covering paper and roll the ink smoothly over its surface, re-inking the roller as necessary, until the tile is covered. The drawn lines should stand out white against the ink. Show the children how it should look and remind them that if the lines are not visible, then the drawings are not deep enough.

When the ink is evenly spread on the tile, take the A2 sheet of paper and put it on a clean surface. Carefully pick the tile up, holding it gently by the edges and keeping your fingers out of the ink. Decide where the first print is to be laid and carefully lower it into place. (It is possible to pre-mark the places on to the sheet before you begin, but let the children experiment 'by eye' first to get experience of the process before introducing a restricting element.)

Now press it firmly down, being careful not to slide it or the print will be blurred. Take a clean dry roller and use this opportunity to show the children any particular marking system you have used to indicate clean rollers. Reinforce the need for care of equipment and the appropriate use of special art tools. Then, using this dry roller, roll over the back of the tile firmly and evenly, ensuring that all sections are covered by the action. Then put the roller in a clean place.

Now the magic moment! Very carefully peel the paper away from the tile – be careful as the tiles can be brittle and crack easily if you are too exuberant. The first print will be revealed.

Now re-ink the tile using the same colour and repeat the process placing the second print where you wish the pattern to be repeated. Continue until all the paper is filled. Constantly stress the need to keep inks and inked rollers in safe places and to work as cleanly as possible with dry rollers. If any ink smudges on to a dry roller, ask the children to clean it off immediately with a paper towel. Make sure to demonstrate how any messy covering papers should be

Printmaking 45

removed and thrown in the bin to leave a clean working surface for others to use. Explain how the wet print should be put in a safe place to dry and that the tile can be washed carefully with warm water and retained to use again.

Now ask groups of children to prepare their own prints, helping each other and reminding each other of the process. Younger children will need support but older children should be able to manage the process well. Make sure that at the end of the process the children show their work to the rest of the class and explain how they made their patterns and how they solved any problems they may have had.

When the children have had a chance to make their repeat patterns they can go on to overprint in another colour. Ask them to cut small parts of the tile away using scissors or craft knives under careful supervision. Then let them repeat the printing process, taking care to use a darker colour for their second print and to lower it exactly into place over the original, or to print it slightly off-centre to see what effects can be achieved. This cutting and printing process can be continued many times. Remember to keep the tiles and final prints so they can be displayed together. The children could also write about their work to complete the display. Younger children can dictate their comments!

Further activities
• Use the process to print a row of different houses or homes, or create a town or village in the same way.
• Print decorative borders on a theme to complement a topic or project.
• Print and overprint a huge class picture of trees to make a forest scene.
• Produce class, school or individual Christmas cards or calendars, printing on thin card.
• Print individual invitations to school events.
• Use the printed sheets to make book-covers, backgrounds for posters or other school work.

7. Fabric prints

Objective
To develop the printing process by using fabric.

Age range
Seven to eleven.

Group size
Whole class or groups.

Time
At least two hours, plus an overnight period to allow fabric to dry.

What you need
A large polystyrene tile with prepared design (see previous activity), printing inks, dry rollers, ink rollers, Formica offcuts, squares of fabric larger than the tiles by about 4cm all round (plain light colours in both natural and synthetic fabrics), sewing threads and needles, a collection of beads and trimmings, fabric adhesive, a book of embroidery stitches and designs, foam scraps.

What to do
Use some of the ideas in the previous activity so that the children have some successful experience of printing on paper. Ask the children to prepare another design or develop their original idea further on to a new sheet of polystyrene. If you have sufficiently large pieces of fabric, let the children use a larger sheet of polystyrene for this activity. Follow the directions for printing as described in the previous activity but in this case ask the children to make one really good print on to fabric. Make sure that they have used sufficient ink to cover their tile thickly and evenly. It is also essential that children should help each other during the printing process, with one or more stretching the fabric taut while the printing is going on. After printing, the fabrics should be left to dry and the printing materials cleared away.

Leave the fabrics to dry overnight, then allow the children to look at their work. Overprinting is possible at this stage or the children can work directly on to the single print. Explain that they can now embroider their designs with a range of stitches to make their designs more interesting. If possible, let them look through examples of stitches to give them a range of possible ideas. Let the children choose the colours of their embroidery threads and discuss them before they commence work. Ask them why they have chosen particular colours and how they will use them. Try to get them to think through design possibilities rather than randomly selecting materials. If they want to develop a particular idea, such as a theme on shades of one

Printmaking 47

colour, and materials are not readily available, encourage them to search at home so that they can develop their ideas rather than become restricted by the only range available in school. Ask children also to select the beads and trimmings with the same overall planning in mind. It might be useful for you to restrict choices to particular colours to encourage a more analytical use of materials. If you are introducing the use of beads, remember that young children can be like magpies with beads and will often choose the most glittery examples because they are naturally drawn to them! Try to encourage discerning choices for particular effects.

If you are working with young children, it will be easier for them to stick many of their threads and trimmings in place. Threads can be cut into tiny pieces as necessary and stuck on to resemble stitches to give special texture where young fingers cannot manage sewing skills. Encourage the children to seek out examples of embroidery and textile design that will help give them ideas. There are some excellent links with history here. For example, the wall hangings and curtains and bed-hangings of the Tudor and Stuart period or historical costume design could form an inspiration point. The designs on jewellery and patterns on pottery from the Viking and Roman periods may suggest ideas, as may other artefacts from different times and cultures.

When the designs are completed they can be stretched over card (Figure 1) and mounted to form panels. They can also be sewn together with another similarly sized piece of fabric, then stuffed with foam pieces or scraps, to make a decorative cushion. Alternatively they can be sewn together to make a class wall-hanging or curtains for use in school. They can also be stuck to thick paper, using a strong PVA adhesive, and used to make book covers. Ask the children for their ideas as they are bound to have a rich fund of suggestions.

Further activities
- Prepare your own equivalent of the Bayeux Tapestry, by joining together small sections depicting consecutive events in one long line around the classroom.
- Sew the prints together to make a canopy to cover a corner of the room.
- Sew the prints together and present it to an old people's home, hospital ward or library as part of a community venture.

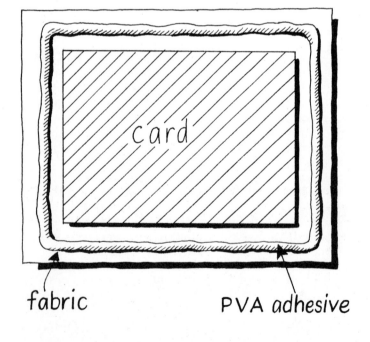
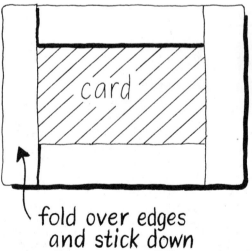

Figure 1

CHAPTER 4

Ceramics

A large amount of the earth's surface is composed of clay. Children will already be familiar with many of its uses, for example, cups, plates, mugs, bricks and sinks etc. It was even used on the outside of the space shuttle to help deflect the heat on re-entry to the earth's atmosphere. It is used all over the world and in every culture to make both everyday artefacts and also special items of exceptional beauty. It is cheap, user-friendly and already available in most schools.

• There are a number of curricular areas which can be covered by work in ceramics. For example, the word 'ceramic' comes from the Greeks. You may already have looked at Greek pots for their shape and decoration as part of history and geography.

Work in ceramics is also useful for introducing earth sciences. (For example, clay is formed as a result of glacial action over an extensive period of time. Glaze is made from silica and other substances which are also taken from the earth.)

Ceramics 49

BACKGROUND

It is possible to buy ready-to-use clay by the bag-full. Clay like this will hold its shape well either for 'throwing' on the wheel or for making hand-built ware. It can be a liquid state – called 'slip' – which can be coloured, used for casting into plaster moulds, for decorating ware or for joining pieces of clay together.

The process of claywork is fairly simple. Finished items need to dry out until bone-dry before firing in a kiln for the first time. This first firing is called bisque firing and makes the work permanently hard, although not waterproof. A second firing following glazing – a thin coating of glass painted on to the clayware – is needed to render it waterproof. The thin coating of glass fuses to the ware and seals it in the gloss firing.

Bisque firing

The kiln can be packed with work touching each other. Some small items can be placed inside larger ones to make full use of the space available. Tiles can be stacked on top of each other but care must be taken not to put too much of a load on to fragile work which could break under accumulated weight. Remember that if work breaks at this stage it cannot be joined together again with slip. The last stage for slip joining is when clay is 'leather-hard', ie. when it is not completely dried out.

When the kiln is packed, the door must be carefully closed and the 'bungs' removed from their holes. (There is usually one in the door and one at the top of the kiln.) Put the input regulator to low and set the temperature to 980°c. Switch the kiln on, taking care to use the input regulator to keep the rise in temperature slow, until it reaches 400°c. Then put the bungs firmly back in place and set the input regulator to maximum. When the temperature reaches 980°c, the kiln should be switched off and allowed to cool. This may take some time, so be patient. When it is cool and safe to touch, the kiln can be unloaded.

50 Chapter 4

Try to keep to a minimum the delay between bisque firing and glazing and gloss firing. Too much handling, especially by small hands, can result in greasy fingerprints which acts as a resist to glaze. Also, long delays and storage allows dust to settle on the ware which can give all sorts of problems later. If possible, it is best to unpack the kiln from the initial firing and decorate the work with glaze immediately, finishing it completely with a gloss firing.

Gloss firing

With gloss firing it is essential that the work does not touch any other piece and no glaze should come into contact with the shelves – called 'bats'. The 'bats' should have been prepared with a coating of 'bat wash'. If the shelves appear white on one side this has been done. If this is not the case, order a small amount of 'bat wash'. It comes in a powdered form and should be mixed with water and painted thoroughly on to the 'bats'. After the first firing this coating turns white and offers some protection for the 'bats' if any glazes run on to them.

When the kiln has been carefully packed and the door firmly closed, you will need to select the temperature. Check the firing instructions on the glazes you have used as they vary, but in general they will range from between 1080°c and 1100°c. A much hotter and swifter firing is needed for this gloss firing. Leave the bungs in this time. Set the input regulator to maximum and switch on the kiln. When the set temperature has been reached, switch off the kiln and allow it to cool. Again, have patience as this may take up to two days this time!

It is always exciting unpacking the kiln after a gloss firing to see what colours and effects have resulted. It is useful to experiment with different glazes and do some test pieces, keeping notes on how you have prepared them. These can then be kept for future reference and can help children decide on the effects they would like to achieve.

Glazes

Glazes are usually bought ready prepared in an easily used powdered form. They are mixed with water according to the instructions and then painted on to the bisque-fired claywork using broad brush strokes. However, brush-on glazes can be purchased; these are very easy to use. They come in plastic bottles ready for immediate use. For really good coverage it is recommended that three coats of glaze are utilised, allowing each coat to dry thoroughly before adding the next.

ACTIVITIES

1. Pinch pots

Objective
To introduce a simple way of making hand-built pottery.

Age range
Five to eleven.

Group size
Small groups.

Time
30 minutes.

What you need
Ball-shaped piece of clay for each child (in good workable condition – neither too hard nor too soft), assortment of objects for making patterns, overalls.

What to do
If this is the first time clay has been used, demonstrate the technique of making a pinch pot. Take a piece of clay about the size of an egg and use your thumb to push a hole into it, while holding the ball of clay in your other hand. Explain that the children should not push the hole all the way through. Show them how to 'pinch' out the clay by keeping your thumb in the

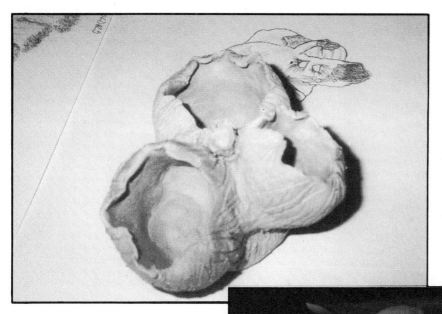

clay and spreading your fingers round the outside, continuing to work round the rim of the pot by pinching and turning it in your hand, creating a rhythm. Explain that this procedure should not be rushed – concentration is necessary. The thickness of the clay wall should be about 5–8 mm thick.

Let the children try to make their own pinch pots. Be aware that there will be a tendency to pinch the walls of the pot too thin (this is to be avoided as it is likely to collapse) or not to push the thumb deep enough into the bottom of the pot (so it will become too thick).

As the bowl progresses, encourage the children to bring the clay towards the centre (ie. the thumb) using their fingers to control the size of the opening, otherwise it is likely to become too big. At this stage, some children may wish to transfer the bowl to the table so that they can work with both hands.

When the pot is completed, let the children press objects on to the pot to make patterns. Make sure they put their initials on the bottom of the pot for later identification. Completed pots should then be stored to dry out before firing.

Stress that at the end of the session it is important that all tools, equipment and working surfaces should be cleaned and any unused clay correctly stored in bins or polythene wraps. Make sure that the children wash their hands afterwards.

Further activities
• Two pinch pots can be joined together with 'slip' to be formed into animal shapes.
• When clay is a little harder, interesting shapes can be cut into the walls of the pot.
• A small foot can be added to the base using slip.
• Look at the work of Lucy Rie or Mary Rogers (potters who have used the pinch pot technique in their professional work).

2. Wrap-around pots

Objective
To continue simple pot-making, including introducing slab pottery.

Age range
Seven upwards.

Group size
Small group.

Time
30 minutes.

What you need
Clay, rolling-pins, boards or protective covering for tables, overalls, slip, yoghurt cartons, modelling tools, wooden battens, paper towels or newsprint.

What to do
Give each child a piece of clay the size of a grapefruit, a board, rolling-pin and battens. (If necessary, you can make these from offcuts of wood, 30cm × 2–3cm, with a thickness of about 5–10mm.) Let them share tools, rulers, a yoghurt carton of slip and an extra rolling-pin.

Ask them to roll out the clay on to a paper towel or newsprint (it will stick to a Formica or plastic surface). Show them how to turn the clay over and round by moving the battens around and using both hands as the circle of clay becomes larger and flatter. Explain that they should finish with a rough pancake shape rather than a tongue of clay.

Using a batten as a straight edge, demonstrate how to cut off a piece of two connecting edges to form a right angle as in Figure 1.

Next help them to wrap a paper towel or piece of newsprint around the rolling-pin. Make sure that no clay is stuck to it and that the paper is level with the bottom of the rolling-pin (Figure 2). Then show the children how to put the paper-wrapped rolling-pin on one of the straight edges of

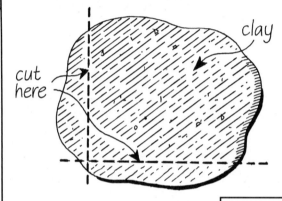

Figure 1

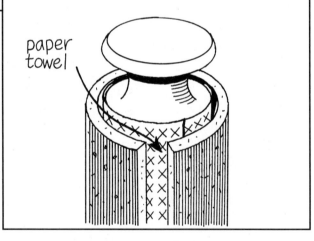

Figure 2

54 Chapter 4

clay and roll the clay around the rolling-pin until the clay overlaps by about 5mm (Figure 3), then carefully cut off any excess clay. Ask the children to keep this as it may be used for the base later.

Ask the children to stand the rolling-pin on end with the clay on it, supporting it with one hand. Show them how to work from the bottom up to seal the clay with a finger. The sealed edge can be tidied with a modelling tool. Get the children to cut carefully around the top until it is level. By this time there should be a sealed cylinder of clay wrapped round a covered rolling-pin which is standing on its end. If there is enough excess clay, let them use it to make bases for their pots. If not, let them roll out a piece of clay the same thickness to make a base. Show them how to pick up the rolling-pin carefully with the clay wrapped round it and place it on the rolled out clay near the edge (Figure 4). This will make it easier to cut. Show the children how to cut a circle around the cylinder with about 5mm extra allowance, then take away any surplus clay. Ask them to mark with a tool around the edge of the base and also around the bottom of the pot as in Figure 5. Get them to put slip on both marked edges, then place the cylinder on top of the base, before pressing down so that the slip oozes out. Make sure they clean up any surplus slip. Now ask the children to use a modelling tool to join the 5mm overlap on to the cylinder and roll all the way round, making a neat join. Stress that during this time the children should not put any weight on the rolling-pin, otherwise it will push through the base.

Any remaining clay can be used to practise pattern-making using different tools. A favoured

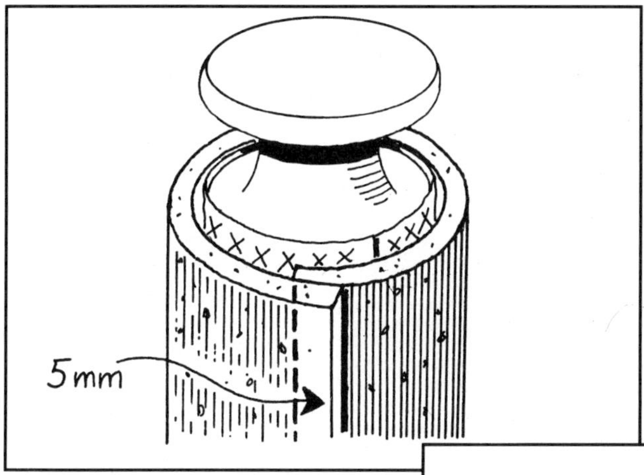

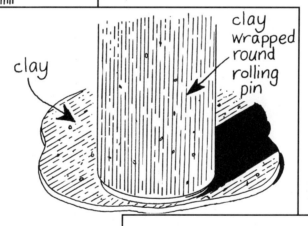

Figure 3

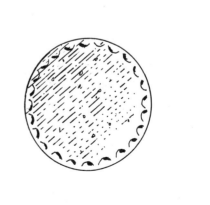

Figure 4

Figure 5

Ceramics 55

design can then be transferred on to the sides of the pot. Then the rolling-pin and the paper towel should be removed leaving the pot free. If the paper is stuck inside it does not matter as it will burn out in firing. However, if the rolling-pin is left in too long, the clay will shrink on to the rolling-pin and is likely to crack.

Often there is a sharp edge on the top of the cylinder, in which case, ask the children to smooth it down with a modelling tool or finger before firing.

Stress the following points when the children have finished working.

• The pot should be marked for identification and stored away prior to firing and glazing.
• After each session, all surplus clay should be scraped up and put into appropriate containers.
• Tools, equipment, working surfaces should be cleaned at the end of the lesson.
• Pupils must wash their hands after everything has been cleaned and put away.

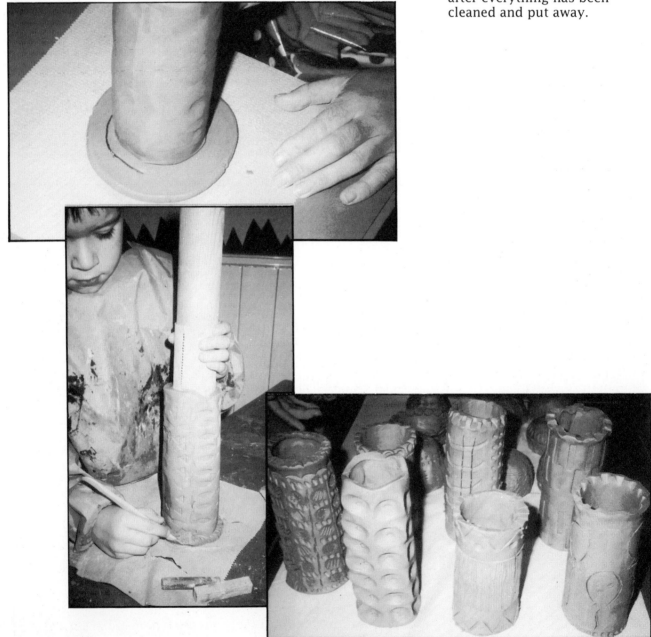

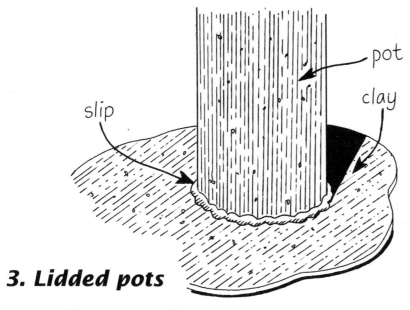

3. Lidded pots

Objective
To develop the technique of wrap-around pots (see previous activity).

Age range
Seven upwards.

Group size
Small group.

Time
30 minutes.

What you need
Unfired wrap-around pots from previous activity, polythene bags or bin liners, rolling-pins, boards, modelling tools, pair of compasses, overalls, clay, slip, wax, brushes, glaze, kiln.

What to do
After the children have made wrap-around pots (see previous activity), ask them to put their work aside for a day or two, wrapped in a polythene bag. Whole groups' work can be put on a board and wrapped in a bin liner. Care will need to be taken so that the pots do not dry out too much. (On a hot summer's day they could dry out within

Figure 1

a few hours.) They need to be leather-hard.

Ask the children to roll out enough clay to make a lid for the pot and to secure it to the top of the pot with slip (Figure 1). Remind them to score both edges and to apply slip to both surfaces. Get them to trim the lid so that it fits exactly, then clean off excess slip.

Now ask the children to mark a wavy line lightly about 3 or 4cm from the top (Figure 2). Explain that it should not be too deep. When they are happy with it and the line goes all the way round, let them cut through the clay until the lid comes off. This can be done with the end of a point from a pair of compasses or any sharp instrument. Explain that they should do it gradually, turning the pot round each time, gradually increasing the depth of the compass point. When the pot is pierced and the lid is free, encourage the children to clean all edges and use the opportunity to seal the inside of the lid.

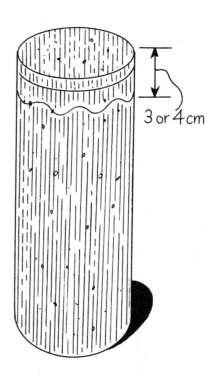

Figure 2

Let the children make patterns on their pots with modelling tools, or roll out thin pieces of clay and arrange them on the pot, sticking them firmly in place with slip. Make sure they put their initials on the underside of the pot. The pot can then be glazed and fired.

Explain that while the lid needs to stay on the pot during drying and firing, extra care must be taken to make sure that there is no glaze on the edges or the lid will stick to the pot. This can be avoided by painting a film of wax (from the batik pot perhaps) on both edges before glazing. The lid may still be reluctant to come off the pot after firing, but a sharp tap or two will usually release it.

4. Candle-holders

Objective
Further developments of wrap-around pots.

Age range
Seven upwards.

Group size
Small group.

Time
30 minutes.

What you need
Wrap-around pots (from Activity 2), overalls, pencils, paper, scissors, pair of compasses, candles.

What to do
In this activity, the children are going to make a candle-holder where the base will hold the candle and the negative spaces will let out the light.

Give the children their leather-hard pots and discuss the various shapes that could be cut into them to turn them into candle-holders. Encourage the use of words such as circle, diamond and lozenge. Explain that if too many shapes are cut out, the pot will collapse.

Get them to draw their shapes on paper, cut them out and place them on their pots, about 4 to 5cm from the bottom. When they are happy with their arrangement, ask them to check that there will be enough clay left to support the rest of the pot when they cut the shapes out. Get them to cut carefully round the paper shapes with a sharp modelling tool, gradually going deeper until they have gone through the pot, then let them gently remove the shapes. Ask them to clean the edges of the holes to leave them smooth.

Next ask them to draw a wavy line all round the pot about 2 to 3 cm from the bottom. Ask them to draw lightly at first, checking that the line meets and that there is not too 'pointed' a shape, as these are easily broken. Let them gradually cut deeper until they pierce all the way round and the pot can be separated into two pieces.

Explain that the children will need to tidy up the edges and that both pieces of the pot must stay together during drying and firing. Care must be taken with glazing (see previous activity).

CHAPTER 5

Textiles

Children should be given opportunities to explore and begin to understand the different properties of a range of materials. This links well with the demands of science and technology in the National Curriculum as well as art – which requires not only experience of working with a variety of materials including textiles (AT1, Investigating and making) and also the use of varied tools. It is useful for schools to build up a collection of fabrics as a source of investigation. For instance, in addition to a 'bit box' full of varied scraps sent in from home, schools could start to collect varied textile lengths which could also be used as drapes to embellish displays and create attractive and interesting environments. Parents and friends will often provide the school with suitable threads and textiles in response to a gentle letter home.

Textiles 59

BACKGROUND

Any collection of fabrics should include both natural and synthetic textiles, such as cotton, linen, wool, nylon, polyester, polythene, etc. There should be examples of different colours and colouring techniques such as unbleached calico and natural wools; dyed or printed; woven or knitted; plain and patterned. Aim to provide a good range of differently constructed specimens such as mesh, finely woven, loosely woven, machine knitted, felted and continuously extruded or manufactured 'sheet' materials like plastics and tinfoil.

It is important to include materials of other than white European origin. Here is an exciting opportunity to look at some of the wonderful multicultural fabrics available. Batiks and colourful prints with traditional patterns are fairly easy to obtain and often local markets and Asian shops will be a rich source of such finds at a bargain price.

In addition to the aesthetic qualities of the materials, children should consider the functional aspects – waterproof or otherwise, suitability for use, ease of cleaning etc. These are all essential elements in the design process. Sometimes this knowledge can be used in reverse to deconstruct fabrics to create something that gently shocks and stirs the imagination (see Activity 3).

Any investigation into the properties of fabrics will stimulate a rich language response. It can be very effective to display fabrics with labels attached containing the descriptive words chosen by the children. For instance, a

length of delicate sari material might produce labels very different from an adjoining fall of thick polythene sheeting.

The best way to store fabrics is either folded in a cupboard or on hangers on a rail. They can be grouped according to colour, style or manufacture. In fact, the very activity of finding ways to sort and classify them is a valuable learning experience in its own right!

Similarly, knitting yarns and sewing threads should be colour sorted. The best way to do this is to buy a number of cheap raffia wastepaper baskets and to ask children to colour sort the yarns and threads into these bins. These are then easy to transport to any work area, easy to select from and look lovely in their own right wherever they are stored in a classroom. They can even make an attractive display which doubles as a storage place!

It is also useful for a collection of beads, feathers, shells and other trimmings to be made. These can be sorted and stored in clear plastic containers. Pop bottles with their tops cut off work well.

Although it is important that all children have opportunities to sew and use threads, sometimes extra embellishment is needed which is better effected by gluing, therefore adequate fabric adhesives will be required from time to time. Children also enjoy learning to create new fabrics by weaving, knitting and knotting threads. Wherever possible, they should also be allowed to sew using a sewing machine, preferably an electric machine with a retarder gear that will prevent the children accelerating out of control! (Hand machines can be valuable but it is much more difficult to control feeding the fabric through using only one hand.)

Textiles **61**

ACTIVITIES

1. Wax resist

Objective
To introduce the idea of wax resist work.

Age range
Five to eleven.

Group size
Small groups or class.

Time
30 minutes.

What you need
White household candles, dark coloured sugar paper, white paper, pots of watery paint, thick paint brushes.

What to do
Ask the children to use a candle as a mark-making tool to draw on the dark paper. Explain that their drawings should show up fairly well against the dark background and encourage them to experiment with dots, squiggles and lines (see Chapter One, 'Drawing and mark-making'). When the children are happy with a particular pattern or design, ask them to keep their designs for reference and use the candle on the white paper to draw out the chosen shapes. This can be quite tricky as it is hard to see the wax lines. Ask the children to ensure they use all their paper. (You have an excellent opportunity at this point to talk about negative images and opposites, see Chapter Three, 'Printmaking'.)

When the design is complete, let the children use the watery paint to paint over the total paper area with large brush strokes. The wax resist should then be revealed giving exciting results.

Let the children repeat the exercise using different coloured washes to compare the effects.

Further activities
• Restrict the choice of design to letter shapes (see Chapter Seven, 'Graphics'). These can be single letter shapes or repeated shapes to make decorative borders or word patterns. These wax resists could be used as a background mounting for children's writing or to cover class work books.
• Let the children make a maths wax resist, using figures, symbols or shapes as the design. This will help to reinforce correct formation.
• Make a 'magic carpet' by taping together the finished squares. Let the children cut out a paper fringe and stick it to opposite edges of the complete work to make it look like a huge mat. The children can stick on painted characters and write stories describing the adventures of the travellers. The whole magic carpet would make a spectacular display, either wall mounted or suspended in flight!

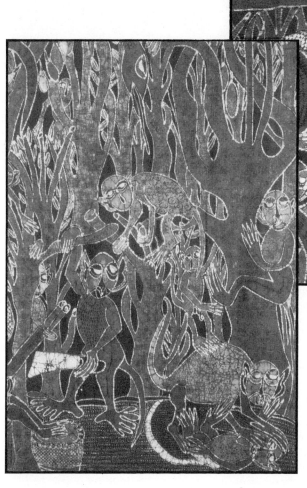

2. Batik

Objective
To learn simple batik techniques.

Age range
Nine to eleven.

Group size
Small groups or individuals.

Time
At least one hour.

What you need
Examples of batik, an electric batik pot (which requires no water and is thermostatically controlled), about 300gm wax flakes, old stiff round brushes, a selection of tjanting tools (holders with small piped reservoirs), covering paper, clean light coloured cotton or polyester fabric, selection of fabric inks or paints, cold water dyes and dye bath, masking tape, large empty ice-cream tub and large elastic band (optional), board or Formica table, pencil, cooker and old preserve pan or iron and absorbent paper.

What to do
Explain to the children that batik work simply means decorating a fabric with a wax design which will then resist absorbing any further colour which might be applied, either by immersion in dyes or by being painted on to the cloth. When the process is completed the wax 'resist' is removed by applying heat which melts the wax out of the material and leaves lines and patterns on the original fabric unmarked by added colours.

Tell the children that the results can be very simple or highly complex and are common textile decorations throughout the world. Beautiful examples of this craft can be seen in fabrics from Asia and Africa (where the resist can be particular sorts of river mud). Very often the designs include illustrations of local wildlife as well as floral and traditional patterns. It would be useful if you have some examples to show them, or perhaps illustrations or postcards.

Before allowing the children to make their own batik, demonstrate the process as follows. Site the batik pot safely where it cannot be accidentally knocked over and where the electric lead is secure. Shake enough wax flakes into the pot – usually a minimum line is indicated – and switch it on, then wait until all the wax has melted. Encourage the children to watch this action and draw their attention to the scientific process. At this stage the wax will be hot and children must be taught to observe simple safety precautions.

Next cover a suitable surface, such as a board or Formica topped table, with several layers of paper or a polythene sheet. Take a clean piece of fabric, about 30cm square, stretch it and fasten it securely with masking tape or similar, so that it remains taut. Alternatively, stretch the fabric across a large ice-cream tub and secure it with an elastic band.

Lightly mark in pencil guidelines for any design you wish to follow. Now dip a brush into the wax and, working very quickly before the wax sets, draw around your design making sure that the wax has soaked into the fabric. Experiment with dots, lines, wiggles and fill in small shapes. You will find that the wax will solidify quickly on your brush, in which case simply return it to the pot for a minute and it will be ready to use once more.

Dip the reservoir of a tjanting tool into the hot wax, keeping the pipe uppermost to retain the wax safely inside. Carefully turn the pipe over so that the wax can flow out and trail it along the line of your drawing. You will find that you can draw for some time before the wax hardens and that you can achieve fine, well-controlled lines. To re-melt the wax, merely place the tool back in the batik pot.

Let the children experiment with different sized tjanting tools and note the effects that can be made. When they have finished, leave the wax to harden and switch off the pot. Any brushes used can be left in the pot to set in the wax

until next used (they can not be used for any other activity). The tjanting tools can be emptied and set aside.

When the wax design is set hard, let the children use good quality fabric paints to help you paint in colour sections, brushing each area separately or boldly brushing across the wax lines as you please. If you have chosen large blocked wax shapes, let the children experiment with cracking the wax with their fingers and then trailing the paint so that it seeps through the fractures. Alternatively, prepare a bright cold water dye in a suitable container, and immerse the fabric in the dye-bath. (This can be very effective if you want an all over colour effect.) Fix and rinse the dyed fabric according to the maker's instructions and leave it to dry thoroughly.

When the fabric is completely dry there are two methods of removing the wax to reveal the original markings. One way is to boil the fabric in a large, old container such as a jam pan until the wax runs out. However, this is

dependent on the colour-fast properties of your paints or dyes and is also extremely messy. A much easier method is to place the fabric on a thick wad of paper and cover it with several more sheets of absorbent paper, such as sugar paper, newsprint etc. Heat an iron to a very hot setting and keep running it over the top papers until the wax melts out of the fabric and into the paper. When the paper becomes too soaked with wax replace it with fresh paper and repeat the ironing process until you have removed as much of the wax as possible. (Naturally, with young children an adult should always perform this operation.)

Remove the fabric (which will still feel a little stiff) and reveal the completed batik! Before discarding the papers you have used for ironing, hold them up to the light – you may also have captured a very interesting wax design image which can be displayed against the windows!

64 Chapter 5

3. Textured textile collage

Objective
To investigate the construction of different fabrics.

Age range
Seven to eleven.

Group size
Whole class or groups.

Time
At least one hour.

What you need
Designs or illustrations of animals (for example, Rousseau's jungle pictures), paper, pencils, large sheets of thick sugar paper or similar, scissors, PVA adhesive, spreaders, collection of fabrics, especially thicker heavyweight materials such as woollens.

What to do
First of all ask the children to look at reproductions of pictures of animals. Rousseau's jungle paintings are ideal. Ask them to choose a bird or an animal and make a preliminary drawing of it. Encourage them to talk to each other about their reasons for this choice. Ask them to tell each other about the colours of the fur or feathers and the textures (rough, smooth, tousled, stiff; creamy, dappled, spotted, shades of brown etc.). Encourage them to develop fully the descriptive language.

Using their initial design as reference, get the children to draw a large outline of their bird or animal taking up the entire sheet of sugar paper. Next ask them to select some pieces of fabric which match the colours, or give an impression of the texture, of their chosen creature.

Next ask the children to cut small sections of the fabrics (about 10cm × 5cm) and use their fingers to tease out the threads from the woven cloth. Use this as an opportunity to talk about the weft and the warp and the way weaving locks threads into place, or builds up a pattern or texture. (Heavyweight wools and acrylics will unravel easily, finer cloth is more difficult and they may need to cut smaller sections to help the process. The actual dismembering of the fabrics is a very therapeutic process – especially as the children go on to create something beautiful from the apparent destruction!) Tell the children that they need to keep the different threads in separate piles.

Ask the children to apply PVA adhesive to small sections of their large outline and, choosing the most appropriate threads, stick these down firmly. Encourage the children to work carefully and slowly, with emphasis on the choice of suitable colours, to build up their design matching the texture of fur and feathers. This can be a long process but the results will be worth the endeavour.

Further activities
• Let the children design mythical beasts or alien creatures. Encourage them to look at illustrations of medieval gargoyles for inspiration.
• Restrict the children's choice to animals in literature, for example *The Wind in the Willows*, *Watership Down*, *The Owl who was Afraid of the Dark*, 'The Owl and the Pussycat' etc.
• Go on to look at reptiles and insects and let the children use synthetic materials, such as polythene, plastics, foil etc. and compare their properties with those of the fabrics originally used.
• Have fun creating a furry stag-beetle or a smooth cat! Let the children's imagination run riot and encourage them to look at the world in a new light.

Textiles 65

4. Paper weaving

Objective
To explore the construction of a piece of weaving.

Age range
Six to eleven.

Group size
Whole class or groups.

Time
45 minutes.

What you need
Sugar paper in contrasting colours, scissors, adhesive and spreaders.

What to do
Prepare rectangles of sugar paper with parallel cuts from bottom to top leaving the last centimetre uncut as in Figure 1. Older children can be allowed to cut them out for themselves.

Next ask the children to cut strips of contrasting sugar paper slightly longer than the width of the original rectangle. Show them how to thread it through the cut strips (Figure 2). Be sure to explain the 'under/over' process and demonstrate this if necessary. At this point links can be made with mathematics, discussing the concept of odd and even numbers, and encouraging the children to count as they weave. Explain that all woven fabrics are made in this way, although the actual pattern of the woven threads may differ.

Make sure the children slide each woven row up to the top of the paper and ensure that a little protrudes at each end of a line. Let the children continue weaving until all the rectangle is full. Then let the children snip off the excess strips and very carefully put a tiny amount of adhesive on the loose ends to secure them in place. Remember to explain that this doesn't happen with woven threads!

Further activities
• Instead of using straight cuts, ask the children to make wavy cuts which can vary in thickness. Then let them either weave in straight strips or cut varying strips. The effects can be very interesting (Figure 3).
• Let the children use a polythene rectangle and strips cut from different carrier bags. Encourage them to select different supermarket colours to plan a special colour effect.
• Weave strips of fabric, trimmings, old necklaces etc. into a paper rectangle.
• Use other shapes of paper to form the base and let the children experiment. (What would happen if we wove a triangle/circle/rhombus/random shape?) Reinforce mathematical concepts by asking the children to draw the various shapes they have discussed.
• Use the same technique to create paper costumes for a fashion display, such as cloaks, sleeves, headgear, cuffs and belts etc. Let the children work in groups to create one special costume for a nominated model.

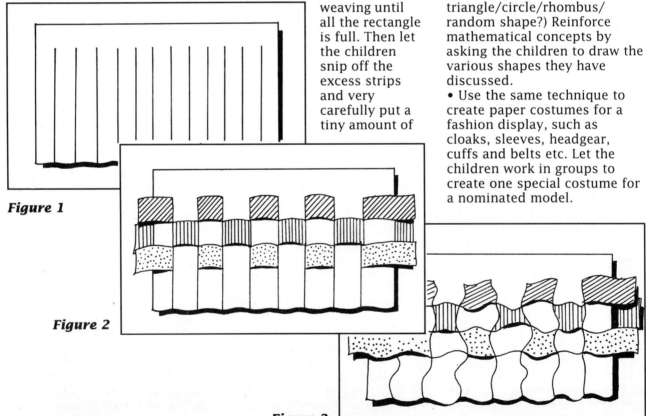

Figure 1

Figure 2

Figure 3

5. Simple loom weaving

Objective
To introduce the use of a loom.

Age range
Five to eleven.

Group size
Whole class or groups.

Time
At least 45 minutes.

What you need
Clean polystyrene trays (such as a take-away or supermarket food tray), scissors, string or thick wool, a range of threads for weaving, plastic weaving needles, trimmings, beads etc.

What to do
Ensure that the children have some experience of basic simple weaving (see Activity 4). Talk to them about looms being used to act as frames for keeping a piece of weaving straight and secure and facilitating the weaving process.

Give the children each a rectangular polystyrene tray and ask them to make small cuts around the edges about one centimetre deep (Figure 1). With young children, you may need to help them or prepare the looms previously yourself.

Using a fairly thick wool, or thin string, demonstrate how to thread up the loom (Figure 2). Then let the children choose their threads and thread up their weaving needles. Remind them of the basic under/over weaving pattern and ask them to weave rows. When they reach the end of a straight row, let them leave

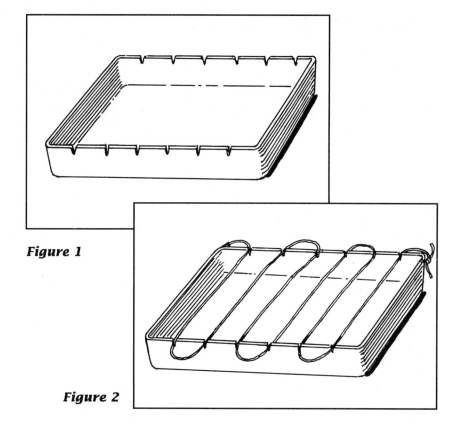

Figure 1

Figure 2

about 10cm over loose and cut off the remainder, then begin a fresh row, or weave back along the next row without cutting the thread, carefully ensuring that they continue with the under/over technique.

Check the children's work carefully as they may omit to weave in the end 'strings' and will be disappointed with their work. Also talk to them about tension and explain that they will pull their weaving into a 'waist' if they pull the threads too tightly. When the children have woven a few rows, ask them to consider incorporating trimmings and ribbons, old necklaces etc. in their fingers, still retaining the weaving technique.

When the weavings are completed they can either be left on the looms for display or, like real weaving, slipped off the loom by gently easing the retaining loops over the polystyrene 'lugs'. If cut ends have been left, these should be knotted at the sides to prevent them sliding out of the weaving.

Further activities
• Use paper plates as looms and let the children investigate ways of threading the loom and then weaving in a spiral.
• Restrict the children's colour choices to shades of the same colour only. Choose 'seasonal' colours and build up a year weaving.
• Join together several pieces of weaving by lacing through the end loops to create a wall hanging. Alternatively hang them side by side, suspended from, or threaded on to, a garden cane.
• Thread small pea-sticks through the end loops and join the sticks together to form cubes, pyramids or other three-dimensional structures.

6. Ladder weaving

Objective
To reinforce weaving skills and knowledge of woven textiles.

Age range
Nine to eleven.

Group size
Whole class or groups.

What you need
A selection of loose-weave fabrics (hessian, woollens, folkweave etc.), scissors, selection of thick threads (wool, thin string etc.), weaving needles.

What to do
Give each child a square of loose-weave fabric. Ask them to look carefully at the weft and the warp and examine how the threads are woven together and any pattern that might be in the weaving itself. Next ask the children to select a thread at least 2cm in from an edge and very carefully, using a weaving needle to help if necessary, remove it from the fabric. Point out the 'ladder' that has been left where the thread was. If the ladder is very narrow, let them tease out an adjacent thread. Encourage the children to choose other threads, either from the weft or warp or both, and pull these out as well. Encourage them to experiment with making random pulls or working out a pattern of ladders.

When the ladders are completed, let the children choose a contrasting thread and weave it into the fabric using their weaving needles. Let them continue until all the ladders are filled. Alternatively they can leave some ladders unfilled and some woven. If the children want to weave in a very thick thread, explain that they will need to remove two or more original threads from the material. Encourage as much experimentation as possible and allow the children to work out a final design, if they wish, on a new piece of loose-weave.

Further activities
• Let the children study different checked or tartan fabrics then ask them to design their own clan material, naming it appropriately.
• Give the children irregular shaped pieces of fabric to work on and fray the edges to keep the shape complete.
• Instead of weaving threads in, let the children add beads, shells, feathers, dried flowers, bark, larch cones etc.
• Restrict the colour choices for fabrics and threads.

7. Plain exploration

Objective
To explore the properties of different fabrics.

Age range
Seven to eleven.

Group size
Whole class or group.

Time
At least one hour.

What you need
Fabric of only one colour (preferably white or cream, unbleached calico is best), ruler, scissors, chalkboard, matching threads or different thickness, assorted needles, coloured paper.

What to do
Cut the fabric into strips of different lengths about 4cm in width. Make the minimum length about 20cm but have some considerably longer. Give each child six strips of different lengths, then ask them to experiment with knotting, plaiting, joining, twisting, slitting, fraying, binding, looping, pleating and fastening each strip until they can produce six totally different worked strips.

Stop the children regularly as they work to compare results. Ask them to describe to the group how they have achieved their 'sampler'. Ask them to choose words to describe the way the fabric has been used and write these up on the board.

Place plain coloured sheets of paper on the floor and, as each strip is completed, ask the children to place them on this base. The sheets can be matching or a chequer-board of mixed colours or, for a really sophisticated display, a match to the samplers! Ask the children all to stand around the display and take turns to choose specimens that are particularly interesting and describe them to see if the others can discover which one they have secretly selected. This encourages speaking and listening skills as well as extending visual awareness. This can be initially difficult but the results are well worthwhile.

Afterwards the samplers can be fastened by one end to a wall-hanging, to a board or a line across the classroom, or down the windows in horizontal rows, to form a textured display.

Further activities
• Ask groups to work in shades of the same colour.
• Ask different groups to use the same colour but in totally different types of fabric.

Textiles

8. Paper adornments

Objective
To use paper to create a textile body adornment.

Age range
Seven to eleven.

Group size
Whole class or groups.

Time
At least one hour.

What you need
Old colour supplements and magazines, scissors, rulers, adhesive and spreaders, threading needles, threads or fine wire, illustrations of Egyptian pectoral adornments or Native American beadwork and jewellery, pencils.

What to do
Show the children examples of beadwork and jewellery from various cultures and compare them. Encourage them to look at colour, design, size of beads and overall shape. (This can form a very useful link in with other topic work such as the Aztecs, Egyptians etc.) Ask each child to cut a long thin triangular shape from a particularly colourful page of a magazine. The triangle should be about 12cm in length and 2cm across the base. Show the children how to wrap the widest part around a pencil and roll the triangular strip up tightly to form a bead shape (Figure 1).

Ask the children to slide the pencil out and carefully unroll the paper. Next get them to spread a small quantity of adhesive along the inside of the curled paper and gently roll it up again to form a bead. (Younger children may still need to roll it around a pencil to hold the bead shape.) Leave the beads to one side to dry.

Encourage the children to make a collection of paper beads, choosing a range of colours which will make their final adornment more interesting. When the children have formed a good collection, let them thread a needle with strong thread or wire (which will make a stiffer structure) and begin to pull the beads together to form a loose necklace big enough to pass easily over their heads. Once the necklace is completed and securely tied, let the children tie on other beads to dangle down in loops or patterns or add other rows of beads. Encourage the children to look at the reference pictures to gather ideas.

Further activities
• Make head-dresses, arm bands, earrings, anklets and belts in the same way.
• Make plain beads which can be painted or sprayed to add interest.
• Add shells, feathers, ribbons, ring pulls, threaded straws etc.
• Restrict the colour choice for different groups to fit in with specific themes, such as the seasons or the four elements (earth, air, fire and water).

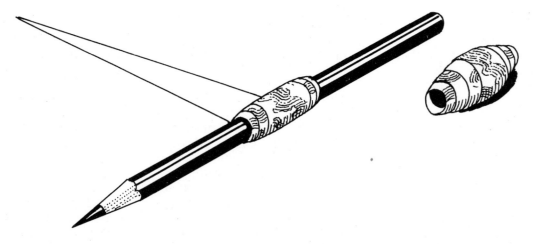

Figure 1

9. Cut lace squares

Objective
To explore the use of spaces within a fabric.

Age range
Nine to eleven.

Group size
Whole class or groups.

Time
One hour.

What you need
A fabric square for each child, sharp scissors, paper, pencils, PVA adhesive and spreaders, a collection of trimmings etc., illustration and examples of lace, collars and ruffs etc., needles and embroidery threads.

What to do
Encourage the children to look closely at the illustrations and examples of lace work. Tell them they are going to produce their own cut work from the squares of fabric, which will not be as fine as lace but which can be based on the same kinds of patterns.

Get the children to draw ideas for designs on paper, experimenting until they find one which will fit on to their fabric and which has spaces in the design which can be easily cut away. Then ask them to draw this chosen pattern on to their fabric square.

Encourage them to use the scissors to cut away the parts of the design they wish to be spaces. If the fabric is likely to fray, explain that they can either deliberately fray the edges of the cuts to make it part of the pattern or lay the completed 'lace' down on paper and carefully paint around the cut edges with PVA adhesive to seal the threads. Point out that if they do this the fabric must be swiftly removed from the paper and hung up to dry before it sticks! Alternatively, the fabric can be laid on contrasting paper, painted with PVA around the cut edges and be left to stick so that the 'lace' shows up against the background. The lace squares can then be embellished with embroidery stitches and beads, or decorated with trimmings, stuck on with adhesive.

Further activities
• Tack all the loose squares together to make a drape, hanging or 'tablecloth' effect.
• Use the stuck-down squares in a display like a patchwork quilt, perhaps to illustrate a suitable story.
• Use the squares to make curtains for a display or younger children's home play area.
• Mount the squares on card and construct three-dimensional structures from them.
• Sew the squares together to produce costumes.

Textiles 71

10. New fabrics for old!

Objective
To create unique fabrics.

Age range
Five to eleven.

Group size
Small groups.

What you need
2 metres of very lightweight iron-on interfacing (Vylene or similar), a large table covered with thick pads of paper or a blanket, an iron, a collection of threads and fabric pieces, scissors.

What to do
Ask the children to look closely at the iron-on fabric and encourage them to feel and look at the little globules of adhesive on the surface. Explain that a hot iron will melt these and that they will bond fabrics together when they cool. Tell the children they are going to invent and design a new material of their own using this iron-on fabric to help them.

Cut the interfacing into two equal pieces. Put one of them on the prepared table adhesive side uppermost. Ask the children to work out some designs by coiling threads to make shapes, cutting and fraying pieces of fabrics to scatter or arranging small pieces of fabric on to the interfacing cloth. Suggest to the children that they design and make some fabric for a special occasion, such as a celebration. Encourage them to experiment and move the threads around until they are quite happy with their design.

Make sure that the children are quite satisfied with their final arrangement and explain that once it is ironed it cannot easily be changed. Lay the second piece of interfacing on top, adhesive side down, then with the iron on its hottest setting, iron and bond the two fabrics together with the children watching from a safe distance. When this is finished, the threads and patterns will be visible through the fine interfacing. The resulting material will be fairly stiff and can be safely cut without fraying. It can be used for a hanging, but spectacular results can be achieved if the children pleat and fold it in interesting ways. It also makes fabulous ruffs, cuffs and collars for Tudor and Stuart costumes!

Further activity
Use this custom-made fabric anywhere a fairly light but stiff and robust fabric is needed (eg. kites, flags, markers, wings, etc.).

CHAPTER 6

Sculpture

We are surrounded by all sorts of sculpture in our daily lives – in our homes, in the streets, parks and shopping precincts – yet this is an area of art that is often overlooked in school. Three-dimensional art is generally very sparse in primary schools. Most children enjoy making models and the classrooms often reflect this, so it should be fairly easy to extend this work into meaningful sculpture experience. The National Curriculum programme of study for Art requires children to:
• Explore and use 2D and 3D media working on a variety of scales (AT1);
• Identify in the school and locality the materials and methods used by artists, craftspeople and designers (AT2).

Study of sculpture can also give excellent opportunities for cross-curricular links with history and geography plus a wealth of multicultural links. Children will be excited and fascinated by sculpture and probably will be surprised at some of their discoveries, such as the fact that the tools and implements used over the ages to shape resistant materials, such as wood and stone, have hardly changed. It may also surprise them to learn that most early statues were designed to be painted – or even dressed!

Sculpture 73

BACKGROUND

The techniques of sculpture will be of great interest to children. Explain how sculptors working on great blocks of stone or wood often prepared for their work by drawing images on all sides and using these as guidelines. In fact, in an effort to ensure accuracy, early sculptors often used a pointing machine. This was a framework comprising carefully placed marker rods which indicated the exact positions for cutting and working. Master craftsmen in the Medieval period also sometimes allowed their apprentices to do some of the preliminary hard work before they began the precision sculpting.

Sculpture may be free-standing or in relief, that is projecting out from a background. Relief may be low or bas-relief (a small projection) as in Assyrian or Egyptian work. It can also be high-projecting as in the Greek Parthenon. Sculpture has traditionally been carved in stone or wood, or modelled in clay and then fired or used to make a casting in bronze. These techniques are still used today, but there have also been exciting developments in the use of modern materials and combinations of materials such as welded metal, fabric, glass, aluminium, stainless steel, vinyl, fluorescent lighting, concrete, fibreglass etc.

In looking at sculpture we bring another range of senses into play and although few, if any, galleries actively encourage visitors to touch the exhibits, the tactile quality of the work is an important element. The rough, smooth or jagged surfaces and textures of sculpture, its sheer size and volume, and its negative and positive spaces invite us to walk around it and explore it from many different viewpoints.

The expressive terms used to describe sculptural forms – dynamic, rounded, tense, fluid, soft, spiralling – extend children's use of language and help develop perceptual awareness of space. It is in fact, the interplay of our senses which helps us to appreciate sculpture and its three-dimensional power. No photograph, however good, can replace the real thing. Apart from galleries, there are many other places where the children can see sculptures. Investigate your local

buildings – particularly civic buildings. They often feature a range of rich embellishment and sculptures which usually reflect the materials in use at the time the building was constructed. A comparison of buildings from different eras would be exciting in historical and artistic terms. For instance, you might compare Victorian statues at the Town Hall with a 60's sculpture at a more modern building, or with fibreglass sculptures at a very new shopping mall. Don't forget the sculptures situated in parks or outside large company buildings, or simple forms of sculpture such as war memorials. A rich source of sculpture can be local churches, both in the actual building, as part of the church furniture (lecterns, pulpits, pews, memorials, statues etc.) and outside on the gravestones (another interesting historical source).

Ask the children to consider how a sculptor works. Although some develop their ideas as they work on their chosen materials, generally artists will sketch, plan and experiment on small-scale work, refining their ideas carefully before they begin the major work. Often they will use earlier ideas and notes from sketch books or drafting books to act as starting points. Encourage the children to work in the same way. In this manner they will work like real artists and may also develop sculptural work inspired by other curriculum areas.

ACTIVITIES

1. Kings and queens

Objective
To introduce pupils to three-dimensional figure work.

Age range
Seven upwards.

Group size
Small groups.

Time
One hour.

What you need
Clay, rolling-pins, modelling tools, sieve, overalls, boards, paper towels, yoghurt cartons containing slip.

What to do
Give each child a piece of clay the size of a grapefruit and ask them to roll it out into a pancake shape about ½ cm thick, then cut out the largest possible triangular shape. Tell them to put any spare clay to one side, then carefully pick up the triangle, using both hands, with the base of the triangle on the board and gradually turn both sides inwards until it forms a cone. Show them how to seal up the centre by pinching the edges together, then get them to cut the point off the cone about 2 to 3cm from the top before tidying up the side join with a modelling tool.

Ask the children to roll a piece of the spare clay into a ball and pinch out a point to fit into the top of the cone. Let them press this into the opening at the top of the cone to form a head and make facial features which they can attach to the head using slip. Hair can be made by pushing soft clay through a sieve. Encourage the children to make a crown for their figures using modelling tools to make patterns before fitting it on the head. Explain that the body of the figure needs to be decorated, so the children should practise on the spare clay to achieve the desired pattern which will be used on the figure body. Suggest to them that the richer the design, the more exciting it will be.

Show the children how to roll out two sausage shapes for the arms. Explain that these will need to be attached to the body with slip, but first some discussion needs to take place as to their position and relative length and thickness. Tell the children how the arms need to be 'offered' to the body to ascertain the correct position. Once this is decided, ask them to mark the position on the body before scratching the surface of the top of the arms and body where they will join together, applying slip and sealing them. Then ask them to tidy the joint and remove any excess slip. Show the children how to bend the arms in front of the figure and

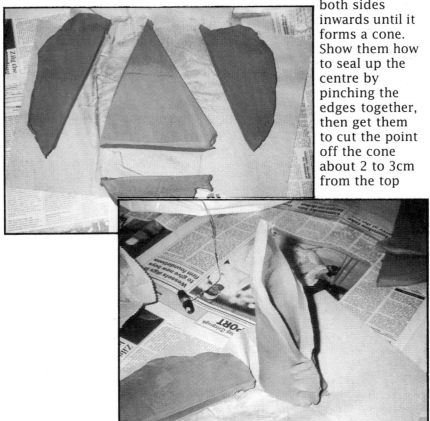

Sculpture 75

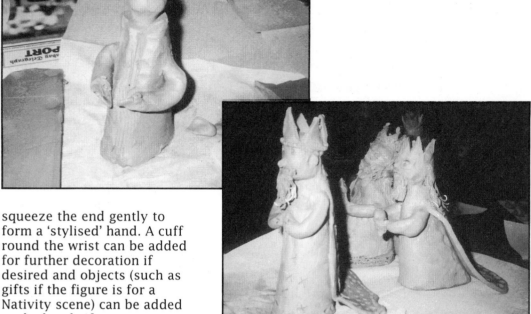

squeeze the end gently to form a 'stylised' hand. A cuff round the wrist can be added for further decoration if desired and objects (such as gifts if the figure is for a Nativity scene) can be added to the hands if necessary.

Let the children roll out a long thin piece of clay about ½ cm thick for a cloak, making sure that it is long enough to trail behind the figure. Encourage experimentation with various shapes (eg. tongue-like, semi-circular, triangular etc). Explain that this should also be richly decorated with pattern. Let them attach the cloak to the back of the head of the figure by 'scratching' and applying slip as before. Explain that the hem of the cloak should rest on the board. Make sure the children mark their work with their initials to ensure easy identification. The completed figures should be kept on their boards and stored for drying. Any surplus clay should be scraped up and put into appropriate containers, and tools, equipment and working surfaces should be cleaned. Make sure the children then wash their hands.

Note that great care needs to be taken when packing the kiln for firing and glazing. The figure and cloak need to be supported when they are placed on the shelf, otherwise the cloak may break off from the figure.

This activity forms useful links with mathematics, history, human biology and RE.

2. Faces

Objective
To develop awareness of facial features and to introduce the concepts of negative and positive spaces.

Age range
Seven upwards.

Group size
Small groups.

What you need
Pictures of the work of Alexander Calder, children's self-portrait drawings (see page 18), wire, card, PVA adhesive, offcuts of wood.

What to do
Show the children the pictures of some of Alexander Calder's wire drawings. Encourage them to look closely and discuss the way he depicted figures, paying close attention to the faces. Give the children a supply of wire and ask them to make self-portraits using their drawings as reference. Encourage discussion about the different ways of joining features such as eyes or mouths to the main structure of the face.

When they have finished, let the children decide whether to mount them on card with PVA adhesive or to make them free-standing by pushing wire from the neck into an offcut of wood.

3. Figures

Objective
To develop three-dimensional work on human figures.

Age range
Eight upwards.

Group size
Small groups, working in pairs.

Time
One hour.

What you need
Sketch books, pencils, examples of sculptures and paintings of figures, wire, offcuts of wood, pliers, scissors, hammer, nails, overalls, newspapers, plaster bandage such as Mod Roc, bowls, water, clay wash, brushes, water-based paint.

What to do
As a preliminary to this activity, ask the children to make sketches of figures based on close observation. For example, they could look at how groups of pupils stand when talking in the playground. Show them examples of the ways in which artists have depicted the human figure, for example the sculptures of Alberto Giacometti, Degas, Rodin, Matisse and the paintings of Lowry.

Ask the children to choose one of the figures to model. Once the pose has been decided upon, get the children to bend the wire into shape and fix it on to the wooden offcut with nails, having made a loop on the figures foot so it will stand. Ask one child in each pair to hold the figure in place while the other fixes it on to the base. Show them how to hammer the nails halfway into the wood then bend the nail over. Ask them to do this each side of the 'foot'.

Cover the tables with newspaper and ask the children to cut the plaster bandage into a pile of small strips while their hands are dry. Put a small amount of water in a bowl, then show them how to dip the plaster bandage into the water and drag it out alongside the edge of the rim of the bowl to take off excess water. Ask them to wrap the bandage around the figure, working from the bottom up. Tell them that the torso can be bulked out with newspaper if desired. The plaster bandage sets hard quickly so two or three layers can be put on to finish.

If there is not enough time and work has to be carried over for another session, the plaster figure should be lightly dampened before the next layer is added, otherwise there is a danger that the new layer will not stick to the dry one. When the figures are complete, let them dry before allowing the children to apply a finish, such as a clay wash or water-based paint, brushed on and rubbed off to reveal texture, form and shape.

Further activity
Let the children use chicken wire to model the sculptures of animals or figures, real or imaginary, then let them cover them with plaster bandage. Make these sculptures on a large scale and use the to enhance the school grounds.

Sculpture 77

4. Reliefs

Objective
To introduce simple relief-making and the use of plaster of Paris.

Age range
Any age.

Group size
Small groups.

What you need
Clay, modelling tools, overalls, bowls, bucket, soft wire, pliers, plaster of Paris, water, petroleum jelly, polythene bags, clay or tempera wash.

What to do
Ask the children to cover the inside of a bowl with a thin covering of petroleum jelly, as if greasing a cake tin. Explain that this will help to release the plaster from the bowl. When they have done that, let them cover the bottom of the bowl with clay to a depth of 3 to 4cm. Allow the children to use tools, hands, natural or manufactured objects to make impressions into the clay. A simple face, landscape or scene could be drawn in the clay, or a design could be used from one of the other activities.

Estimate the amount of plaster needed to cover the design to a depth of 3cm. Fill the bucket with sufficient water to mix, then gently sprinkle in the plaster until you can see an even layer just below the surface of the water. Gently stir the mixture with your hand until it is the consistency of thick cream.

Help the children to take turns to pour plaster over their designs to a depth of 3 to 4cm. When the plaster is almost set, show the children how to bend wire into a hook and insert it near the edge of the plaster. Explain that this will enable them to hang up their sculptures when they are finished. Once the plaster has set completely, ask the children to turn their bowls over, tap them gently and ease their sculptures out. The sculptures can then be displayed. With experience more elaborate designs can be attempted.

Ask the children to clear away, but make sure that no one pours any plaster down the sink as it will set hard. Also ensure that the clay used for this activity is kept separate from the main clay bin as it may contain bits of plaster. Explain that it should only be used for similar sculpture activities.

Further activities
• If there is plaster left over from this activity, pour small amounts into polythene bags and give them to the children to hold while the plaster sets. When the plaster is hard, let the children remove the bags and explain that they have made another type of sculpture. Allow them to colour their work with a clay or tempera wash before mounting it for display.
• Plaster can also be poured over crumpled newspaper to make other interesting shapes.

CHAPTER 7

Graphics

This chapter addresses the use of lettering, which is an important development for all children, not only for the art element but also for the closer observation of presentation skills.

Practical work with lettering allows children to practise letter formation and experiment with different styles. It also enables them to improve their skills in setting out work, organising displays or making presentations of topic work, making posters and signs etc. It can also be enormous fun and lead to developments in three-dimensional work in a variety of media. The links with English AT3 are obvious, but links with AT2 and the development of reading skills – perhaps through phonic work – can also be exploited.

If possible, work in graphics should include opportunities to work in different media. For instance, children can experiment with a range of felt-tipped pens. They can draw a series of words using different width felt-tipped pens, look at the different effects achieved with chisel-edged and bullet-shaped pens and consider the way letters can be created with italic, round-ended or standard nibs on ordinary ink pens and nylon-ended handwriting pens.

The use of colour can be investigated by looking at a collection of posters and colour supplements, book illustrations or advertising materials. A good example of investigating colour effects in lettering would be an examination of yellow. Children often choose to make letters in titles and posters multi-coloured. However, if yellow is used on a white background it usually seems to fade into oblivion and is very difficult to read from a distance. Help the children to see this for themselves by comparing their work and testing the effectiveness of their designs by pinning them up on a suitable wall and examining them from different viewpoints.

Graphics 79

BACKGROUND

Children could also be shown the beautiful scripts produced by other cultures and from other times. A study of embroidery alphabet samplers or the initial letters designed by William Morris could provide a wonderful link with work on the Victorians. The children could look at Japanese calligraphy brushes and learn how to hold them vertically in order to reproduce the bold characters used in Japanese lettering. These could be compared with Chinese characters and the lovely shapes of Arabic or Indian scripts. Further comparisons could be made with other letter forms such as Greek and Russian.

Historical links could be made with a look at Egyptian hieroglyphs, Roman lettering or Celtic illuminated manuscripts.

Mathematical links could be made by encouraging careful consideration of proportion, estimation of size and precise measuring out of guidelines as a preparation for large scale signs, notices or posters.

ACTIVITIES

1. Lettering and advertising

Objective
To enable children to understand that different letter forms can be selected for different purposes.

Age range
Seven to eleven.

Group size
Whole class or groups.

Time
30 to 45 minutes.

What you need
Pencils, paper, felt-tipped pens, ballpoint pens, and a range of mark-making tools, a collection of printed packaging (for example, crisp packets, sweet boxes, cereal boxes, perfume and toiletry packages), books, examples of logos, chalkboard.

What to do
Give the children examples of packaging to look at and talk about the intended audience (eg. children, adults). Discuss the way designers will select particular designs, colours and letter styles to convey particular meanings and to attract different buyers. Talk about advertisements and company logos, sport emblems, badges and wheel trims etc. Ask the children to analyse the reasons for the designer's choice.

Write a word on the board in a style which matches their meaning, for example the word 'soft' written in cloud-shaped letters. Explain that these are known as calligrams. Let the children use a range of tools to design their own calligrams. Ask them to share their work explaining why they chose their lettering style and shapes.

Mount the work on suitable backgrounds for display.

Further activity
Activity 2 develops this theme further.

Graphics **81**

2. Names

Objective
To investigate letter forms.

Age range
Seven to eleven.

Group size
Whole class or groups.

Time
At least one hour.

What you need
Pencils, papers, card, scissors, adhesive, a range of mark-making tools, paints, brushes, water pots, palettes, examples of lettering.

What to do
Ask the children to draw a freehand circular shape on a piece of paper. Explain that they are going to fit the word 'circle' into their shape. Tell them that the letters can overlap, be upside down, reversed etc. Show them examples of different kinds of lettering for reference. If the children find this difficult, let them draw the word 'circle' separately, cut out the letters and arrange them on paper. There will be many overlays. Encourage the children to look at and discuss the shapes that arise.

Let the children choose either warm colours (you may need to talk about these – red, orange, yellow, pink etc.) or cool colours (blue, green, pale purple, white etc.) and colour in each shape without going over the lines. Encourage them to change the shade or tone for each section (see Chapter Two, 'Painting').

Now give each child a piece of A4 paper. Ask them to fold it in half. Using one half in landscape format, ask the children to arrange their forename in whatever style of writing they choose, overlapping etc., to fill all the space. Ask them to colour it in warm colours. Next ask them to turn the other half sheet round for portrait format and, choosing different letter styles, fill the whole paper with their name as before, colouring it in cool colours.

Further activities
• Repeat the activity using different shapes (eg. rhombus, parallelogram, triangle, square etc).
• Repeat the activity using nouns in the same way.

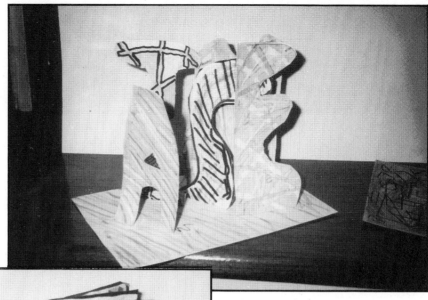

3. 3-D names

Objective
To extend mark-making into three dimensions.

Age range
Seven to eleven.

Time
At least one hour.

What you need
Pencils, card, range of mark-making tools (such as felt-tipped pens, wax crayons, ballpoint pens), adhesive, scissors, children's designs from previous activities.

What to do
Ask the children to use their previous ideas from Activities 1 and 2 to help them draw out their names in separate letters of different styles, about 15cm high. Tell them to draw in an extra 'tab' on the bottom of each letter to allow for sticking the letters down on to a base. Let the children cut these out.

Ask the children to choose another piece of card of a suitable size in relation to the height of the lettering and ask them to arrange their letters in any order, interlinking, overlapping or supporting them as they wish.

This activity is an early introduction to three-dimensional sculpture and the children should be encouraged to turn these arrangements round to study them from different viewpoints. Ask them to look not just at the letters, but the spaces they create between them. Introduce the term 'negative space' to describe these areas. Encourage the children to help each other by holding the letters in place. When they are satisfied with the arrangement, let the children apply adhesive to the tabs and stick the letters on to the card base. Explain that it is useful to stick down only one or two letters at a time, re-viewing and adjusting the arrangement as they add each new letter.

Variation
For the older pupils this process can be developed in ceramics.

4. Snap matching

Objective
To encourage children to look at a whole range of letter styles.

Age range
Six to eleven.

Group size
Whole class or small groups.

Time
45 minutes.

What you need
A collection of colour supplements, discarded books, newspapers, posters and advertisements, A4 paper, paper adhesive, scissors.

What to do
Explain to the children that letters can be made in many different ways for different purposes. Show them a newspaper headline with extremely large letters. Ask them why the letters appear in this way. Show them a small advertisement in a paper or magazine. Discuss the style and appropriateness of the size and layout, ensuring that you explain about the cost of buying advertising space. Encourage the children to scan a range of different newspapers, local and national, to look for the prices for placing advertisements. They could also compare the way a whole range of different advertisements are laid out, such as garage car sales and private car sales. The emphasis should be on the different size and type of lettering used as well as the actual space used.

Then ask the children to select one letter from the alphabet to do a study of the different ways it can be printed or drawn. Give out a selection of papers, advertisements and posters, and ask the children to make a collection of as many different styles of their chosen letter as possible. They should be able to find a great many if they hunt carefully.

Now get the children to cut each example out carefully and arrange their resulting collection to make an attractive pattern of letter shapes on the A4 paper. Do not let them stick them down immediately but ask them to experiment with their patterns until they are happy with their choice. When their pattern is ready, the children can stick them down.

Display and compare their results.

Further activities
• Give the children each a different letter of the alphabet and ask them to produce a complete alphabet line for display and reference.
• Choose numerals instead of letters.
• Choose phonic blends (eg. ing or th) to reinforce reading skills.

5. Positive and negative

Objective
To look at letter shapes in black and white forms.

Age range
Five to eleven.

Group size
Whole class or small groups.

Time
45 minutes.

What you need
Black sugar paper, black and white photographs and illustrations from books and newspapers, white paper, scissors, paper, adhesive, pencils.

What to do
Explain to the children that they are going to experiment with black and white letter shapes on black and white backgrounds. Look at and discuss some examples of black and white photographs in the newspapers and similar illustrations in books.

Give some children a sheet of black paper and others a sheet of white paper. Tell them that this is to be their background. Next give out sheets of both black and white paper to all the children. Ask them to draw really large letters on both sheets of paper. Tell them that these could be their own names, letters forming a sentence, their addresses, the names of class pets or something to do with a class topic. Get them to cut the letters out carefully, making sure some letters are black and the others are white. Next ask the children to arrange their letters on their background sheet so that some of them overlap. Encourage them to do this carefully and to take time making their designs, looking particularly at the effects that can be achieved by putting black over white or on top of a black background, and vice versa. When they are happy with their pattern, let them stick the letters in place.

Further activities
• Choose other colours to repeat the exercise and examine the effect. For example, the children could use opposite colours like red and green or blue and yellow. Introduce the term 'complementary colours'.

Graphics

Alternatively they could use shades of the same colour.
• Do the same exercise with numerals rather than letters.

6. Flights of fancy

Objective
To develop an imaginative lettering style.

Age range
Seven to eleven.

Group size
Whole class or small groups.

Time
At least 45 minutes.

What you need
Paper, chalk board, pencils, pens or writing tools, coloured pencils or felt-tipped pens.

What to do
Discuss with the children the way that letters can be drawn to represent objects. Draw on the board or have already prepared an example of a letter T drawn like a tree or a letter O drawn as a ribbon.

Ask the children to say what other letters drawn in the same style might look like. Let them experiment with these, drawing them about 10cm in height. Encourage the children to compare their ideas and to talk about the differences and similarities. Draw the children's attention to any interesting examples and hold them up for the whole group to see.

Next ask the children to think of other things which could be turned into exciting letter shapes. Make a list of these in a prominent place as a reference point. If you are engaged on a current project consider how this could be linked in to a letter style. For instance, a project on electricity might suggest letters drawn in the form of wires, bulbs and batteries, while a topic on wildlife might lead to animal letters.

Let the children experiment with different ideas and designs and discuss them with their peers to help them make a choice of style. When they have decided on a particular style, ask them to create the whole alphabet in the same way. Stop frequently so that children can show their ideas to the rest of the class and talk about any particular problems they encountered with individual letters and how they overcame the design difficulties.

Further activities
• Ask the children to find appropriate styles to label class displays or to make titles for their own work.
• The alphabets can be created in three-dimensions using card, clay or fabrics.
• The class can design special alphabets to be used by young children in school or for entrance hall displays.

86 Chapter 7

CHAPTER 8

Photography

An increasing number of schools have their own cameras nowadays. Indeed many children are lucky enough to own one themselves. Photography itself seems to be a growing hobby, witnessed by the growth in the number of fast service photography shops in nearly every high street. Most teachers will be familiar with the holiday snaps or records of family events – of widely varying quality – that children bring proudly to school!

Photography can bring an extra dimension to art programmes and, although money must be spent on films and processing, it need not be exorbitantly expensive. The first obvious need is access to a good quality camera. A 35mm automatic camera with fairly robust construction will be the best buy, and shopping around at discount dealers should reveal a range of good quality models at a reasonable price. Such a camera should give good service for many years and be invaluable in recording not just the special festivals and events in a school's life but also the day-to-day life in the classroom as the work of the children develops (the special moments that parents never see). A 35mm camera is recommended because processing is often better value and you can usually get 37 good photographs off a standard 36 exposure film. The only drawback is the fact that you may have a long wait to complete a film if you can only take the occasional shot – and children are always impatient to see the results of their work.

Photography 87

BACKGROUND

Make sure you select a camera with a good built-in flash unit that is easy to use as obviously many of your shots will be taken indoors. The camera should be simple enough for all children to use effectively. Another important feature is to have a camera that will take close-up shots well. Many cheaper automatic cameras will not take clear shots closer than 1 metre distance and yet many of the photographs children will want to take will be of small details, models or natural life. If the camera has a macro facility, make sure this is easy to use.

It is comparatively easy to shop around for good bargains in colour film. Avoid black and white unless you have access to a keen amateur photographer who will process them for you, as processing costs can be very high now that fast service shops are only geared to colour. You might be able to find cheap film near its expiry date and this is usually a good bargain, particularly if you are going to use it very quickly. However, don't buy it if you are going to store it for any length of time. Look out also for the special offers when you can buy 'two for the price of one' but remember to check the expiry date. Always store film in a cool, dry place where it will be safe.

Encourage the children to bring their own cameras to school but make sure that both you and the parents are very clear about who has responsibility for this equipment in case of accidents.

Photography can be used to keep a record of everyday events in the life of a class. Compile a Class Year Book and let the children make an ongoing journal of notable happenings in their class. This might include photographs of

the whole class, together with teachers who work with them and other regular helpers. The children could also photograph visitors to school. Other entries could include:
- class assemblies (including rehearsals and preparations);
- work on science, technology, art and other practical work (often difficult to describe to parents but powerfully recorded with photography);
- children carrying out duties and responsibilities (helping staff, acting as supporters to younger children, serving at a breaktime shop, peer group readers etc);
- work in the school grounds or local visits;
- records of displays of work;
- the development by stages of a school garden or building project.

There are many possibilities. The photographic record can be interspersed with examples of work, poetry, stories, letters and commentaries written by the children on a wide range of events which will give any parent or visitor the flavour of life in the class. At the end of the year, photocopies could be made for individual children and the original book sent to the school library to act as a reference book – and indeed a historical source book for the future. Children love looking back at their past work and it shows a clear record of how they have grown and changed.

Very often parents will want copies of photographs taken by their children. Let them have the negatives and arrange this themselves as single reprints can, for some reason, prove extremely expensive. It is considerably cheaper to order a double set of photographs at the time of processing if you think that there is likely to be a great interest in purchasing extra copies – for individual class photographs for instance. You could add a little extra charge to cover costs and film and let the children organise a mini-enterprise photography sale.

ACTIVITIES

1. Title

Objective
To study portrait photography through practical work.

Age range
Seven to eleven.

Group size
Small groups.

Time
30 minutes.

What you need
A camera with 36 exposure 200 speed film, a selection of 'snaps' and photos, books and magazines showing examples of portrait photography, paper and pencils.

What to do
Tell the children that they are going to look at how photographers take portrait shots. Ask them to look through the selection of examples. Ask them to consider the following questions and write down answers for each of the pictures they choose:
• Is it a close-up shot or a long- or a medium-distance picture?
• How much of the face or body is shown?
• How many people are featured?
• Are there any animals, objects or 'props' used? If there are, why is this?
• What is the person (or subject) doing?
• What impression does the subject give about their character or mood?
• Do the colours in the photograph create any particular effect?
• Where is the light coming from?
• Does the light give a particular effect?
• What time of day is it?

Ask the children to look particularly at the differences between 'snaps' and more composed photographs. Ask them also to look carefully at where the subject has been placed. Introduce the concepts of 'foreground' and 'background'.

Now suggest that they take portrait photographs of each other. Encourage them to try out different ways of doing this, making detailed notes of why they choose certain positions and props etc. Ask the children to choose one of their group to act as a model. Encourage them to work together to experiment with placing their model in a suitable setting, preferably outside in the daylight. (If this is not possible then children will need to be shown how to

90 Chapter 8

use the flash facility.) Ask them to try to take relaxed, uncontrived pictures and to attempt to bring out the character of the model or a particular mood. Suggest that they should try a number of different positions and distances before taking any photos. Ask everyone to decide on one position they really like and to make a careful record of it, including details such as:
• the time of day;
• the direction of the light source;
• the weather;
• the distance of the camera away from subject;
• the exact position of the subject;
• any 'props' used;
• any comments they wish to add.

Let everyone take their turn to take two photographs.

Explain that one should be taken from their original distance and the second one either nearer or further from the subject or alternatively to the left, right or with a higher or lower angle. The purpose of this is to obtain two photographs with minor but perhaps significant differences which may widen the children's compositional experience by offering new viewpoints. Make sure that the children make a record of their second shot in the same way as before and explain that some time will pass before the photos are processed and they will forget the details of their portrait.

Emphasise also that some professional photographers may take dozens of shots walking around a subject, shooting from different heights and angles and using different lighting arrangements to obtain different effects, whereas others will set up an area very carefully in advance to get the composition and special outcome they want. Discuss the different approaches and their different purposes. For example, compare the press photographer, the school photographer, the wedding photographer and the family portrait photographer.

Keep all the notes together safely and explain to the children that they must wait for the processing to be done. When the photographs are returned, ask the children to study their results and discuss whether their original intentions, as recorded in their notes, were achieved.

Encourage the children to try to evaluate each other's work in a positive way, saying what they like about the portraits. Initially ask the 'photographers' themselves to try to suggest ways they could have improved their work. If the children can share in this way and respond thoughtfully and sensitively, then general suggestions for improvements can be made.

Display all the photographs and notes together.

Further activities
• Let the children take photographs of each other to make a whole class portrait gallery.
• Let the children take photographs of the new entrants in the Nursery or Reception classes to make a 'welcome to our school' display.
• The children could photograph all the staff, both teachers and non-teaching staff, to prepare a display for the entrance hall.
• The individual photographs could be used to go on class record folders.

2. Photo montage

Objective
To develop ideas for using photography in collage.

Age range
Five to eleven.

Group size
Whole class or small groups.

Time
45 minutes.

What you need
A collection of photographs cut from magazines or colour supplements, scissors, adhesive and spreaders, A3 paper, reproductions of the photo work of Andy Warhol and similar pop artists, such as Rauschenberg, Oldenburg and Jim Dime.

What to do
Show the children some of the composite pictures made by artists using photographs and collage techniques. Point out the ways in which the artists choose small parts of photos and reposition them to give a different, often amusing or surprising effect. Draw the children's attention to the fact that the photos do not have to be the same way up and can be at different angles or overlapping each other, coloured or black and white. Explain that there are no rules. Now ask the children to choose and cut out illustrations from the selection of magazines. Encourage them to make a substantial pile of

pictures, explaining that they will need enough to cover a sheet of A3 paper. When they have made a good selection, ask them to arrange the pictures on the paper, altering positions to find the most exciting and interesting effect. Older children could be encouraged to decide in advance what sort of effect they wish to achieve. For example, they might want to give an impression of mystery, humour, fantasy or a particular emotion. Ask them to consider carefully the colours they have chosen and how they place one colour against another. For example, if they are trying to produce a strange and mysterious effect, what colours would be best to put together? Ask them to discuss their ideas with their groups. Encourage them to stop from time to time and share the work so far. Finally, when they are happy with their arrangement let them stick the pieces down on the paper.

Further activities
• Restrict the colour choice of available materials.
• Give each of the children different coloured backing paper and compare the different results.
• Restrict the illustrations to objects related to a particular topic.
• Use only real photographs, preferably taken by the children themselves.

3. Time factor

Objective
To use photography to study the effects of time passing.

Age range
Seven to eleven.

Group size
Small group.

Time
20 minutes over the course of a day.

What you need
A camera, paper, pencils, examples of photographic records (such as *An English Forest* by Richard Kraus or *Hill Shepherd* by John and Eliza Forder, see Resources, page 191).

What to do
This activity should be undertaken on a reasonably bright day. Let the children know that they are going to make a photographic record of specific objects over a given

Photography 93

period of time which will show how the weather, light, time of day and other influences might affect photographs.

Show the children photographs of trees, houses or everyday objects which are obviously taken at different times of the day or during very different weather conditions. Ask them to say what they think were the times of day and types of weather in a range of photographs and to explain why they think their choice is correct. Ask them to identify the clues in the pictures that lead them to certain conclusions. Challenge them to look very carefully with questions such as:
• Is it sunrise or sunset?
• What month of the year do you think it is?
• Is the storm beginning or ending?

Explain that the photographers may have taken months to make their collections complete and that they would probably have taken hundreds of photographs but have only selected those that gave the exact impressions they were trying to express. Tell the children that photographers would also keep detailed records of each photograph taken so they could be precise with their information for future reference.

Now ask the children to look around the school grounds and to select a tree, a piece of fixed play equipment, part of a school garden or some other permanent fixture, either within the grounds or close to the perimeter. Let them decide as a group after having looked at a range of possibilities. Next let them come back to the classroom to explain why they have settled on their subject and to discuss any exciting opportunities or problems they might have in photographing it.

Decide together what would be good ways of dealing with these issues. For instance, consider whether it would be a good idea to photograph a bench in the playground at times when it is empty or busy – or a mixture of these. Then decide what times of day would be suitable to take the photographs. Ask the children for suggestions for the best times to give a changing record during the day, such as

94 Chapter 8

the beginning and end of each lesson, or on the hour every hour, or some other specific time period. When the group has decided, get the children to make a list of the times for the photographic sessions and to decide how they will arrange for each one of the group to be able to take a photograph throughout the day.

Ask the children to make a careful note of their chosen subject and to draw a simple sketch plan to identify its position. Stress that each group member should take their photograph from the same position, and that they should carefully record the time, weather and light conditions and any other significant factors. Suggest that they mark the position for the photographer in some way, perhaps by chalking a cross on the playground or pushing a stick into the ground. Let them decide on the best method.

Let other groups do the same exercise but choosing a totally different subject.

When the film is developed, display the range of photographs in chronological order, accompanied by the photographer's notes. Encourage the children to note the changes over the course of a day. Large paper arrows could be used to highlight the differences and explanations could be given if necessary. Alternatively the photographs could be put into a simple homemade book. The children could invent a story to become text to identify the effects over the course of a day. They could call it 'One day in the life of a ....' or choose a more imaginative and exciting title of their own.

Further activities
- Make a photographic record of the same subject at the same time of day for a whole term. This should be very effective in showing a real record of the changing seasons.
- Make a photographic record at regular, predetermined intervals over a longer period of time to record a special project, for example the building of a school extension or an adjacent site, a school garden project or mural etc.
- Make a photographic record each hour of the progress of a model, painting or technological/scientific development in school.

Photography 95

4. Light sources

Objective
To explore the effects achieved by changing the direction of light sources.

Age range
Six to eleven.

Group size
Small groups.

Time
20 minutes.

What you need
A camera, a collection of everyday objects (eg. mug, vase, flowers etc.), a table, a strong torch or light source, measuring tape, paper, pencils.

What to do
Ask the children to choose one of the objects and place it on a table with enough space for them to move around it and look at it from different angles.

Now let one child shine the torch on to one side of the object. Ask the others to describe what they can see. Ask them to look at the very dark areas and the very light areas. Has the light altered the colour in any way? Does the outline shape of the object look different? Encourage the use of vocabulary that will enrich the exercise, such as shadow, light source, direction and angle.

Repeat the exercise with other children holding the torch at different angles and distances from the object. What happens when the light source is directly behind the object? Which areas are dark and light now? What happens if the light is shining directly on to the front of the object? Is the effect different? Why? Now ask the children to hold the light source close to the object. Explain that they are going to take photographs from in front of the object but with the light changing directions. Switch off the flash of the camera otherwise it will nullify the effects of the other light sources. Check the nearest close-up distance from which the camera can take a good photograph and ensure the children understand how far this is. Check by asking them to demonstrate the closest they can go to the object. If the children are very young you might like to measure out this distance with a measuring tape. Older children could be encouraged to practise estimation skills.

Let the children take it in turns to shine the light source as close as possible to the object from their chosen angle whilst another child takes a

Chapter 8

photograph. Ask the children to sketch the outline of their object quickly and block in the areas of deep, medium and lighter tones to act as another record.

When the photographs are developed, encourage the children to study them and compare results. Ask them to identify from which direction the main light source is coming and to talk about any interesting effects. This can form a very useful link with science work.

Further activities
• Repeat the activity using a torch held against different areas of the face of parts of the body.
• Take the photographs outside on a sunny day, turning the object around so that the light falls on different areas.
• Repeat the activity using two different light sources.
• Stand the object on a sheet of clear perspex and try shining the torch from angles below the plastic.
• Stand a mirror to one side of the object, or stand the object on a mirror and shine the light from different high level angles.
• Use this activity with painting rather than photography to introduce mood, atmosphere and tone.

5. Sundial

Objective
To explore different ways of looking at everyday places.

Age range
Five to eleven.

Group size
Whole class divided into pairs.

Time
20 minutes over the course of a day or two.

What you need
A camera, a stick, a flowerpot of soil (optional), chalk or tape, a clock, timer (optional), illustrations of sundials (optional), a large sheet of clear polythene (1m × 1m), a dark spirit-based felt-tipped pen, compass (optional).

What to do
This activity is best suited to a bright sunny day.

Talk to the children about sundials and how they are used to tell the time. If you have any illustrations, show

Photography 97

them to the children and talk about how the sundials function, what they are made of and the sorts of places they can be seen.

Explain to the children that they are going to make their own sundials and make a photographic record of the passage of the sun over the course of a day. Now go out into the school grounds and find a fairly clear space and ask the children to set up a sundial stick. This can either be pushed into soft ground or placed into a flowerpot of soil and stood on the playground. If you choose to use this latter method and have to move it out of the way at breaktimes make sure that the children mark the Tarmac with chalk to fix its position.

Let the children know that every quarter of an hour they will mark the position of the shadow, either by making a chalk mark or by fastening a piece of tape across the ground. Ask for suggestions as to how the tape can be securely fastened down (for example, by using small stones or tiny pegs of wood or plastic). Use the children's ideas if possible. Explain that after marking this shadow they will stand as close to the stick as possible looking along the direction of the shadow. Then they will take a photograph of what they can see ahead of them, acting as if they were the 'eyes' of the sundial.

Divide the class into pairs for this activity so they can help each other, but make sure all children have a chance to take a photograph during the day. It may be necessary to set up two sundials in different places, or continue the activity over two days to give everyone a chance.

Place a clock in a prominent position in the classroom, together with a list of the children's names and times when they are due to check the sundial and take their photograph. Ask the children to check their times carefully and be ready and in place at the right moment. It might be useful to have a timer set up for this purpose, especially with younger children.

Keep a record of the times together with the names of the photographers for future reference. Make sure to take a photograph of the sundials in

98   Chapter 8

their positions and to record the different positions of the shadow marks. This can be done by placing a large sheet of polythene over the top of the chalk or tape markers and drawing in the shadow lines with a dark spirit-based felt-tipped pen.

When the film has been processed, display the polythene sheet with all the photographs arranged in their appropriate position around the edge. The activity can be extended and linked to geography by using a compass to mark the directions on the polythene sheet and carefully plotting the position of the sundial on a map of the school grounds.

6. Close-ups

Objective
To encourage detailed observation and recording of small sections and details.

Age range
Seven to eleven.

Group size
Pairs.

Time
15 minutes.

What you need
A camera, a collection of artefacts related to a specific topic, pencils, paper, coloured pencils, paints or felt-tipped pens, scissors, adhesive, measuring tape, photocopier.

What to do
A camera with a close-up facility is especially useful for this activity as small details can be recorded, but it is possible to record using a camera without this programme provided that the children understand fully the closest they can get to their subject and still take a clear photograph. For young children provide a measuring tape clearly marked with the minimum distance for a successful photograph. Now ask the children to work in pairs to select an artefact related to their topic or other work in progress. Ask them to look at it carefully and to choose part of it to record by photography. Discuss with them appropriate sizes of detail and make sure that they know that very tiny details are unlikely to 'come out' (unless you have a sophisticated camera) and that their picture might be fairly small when processed. Suggest that they look at reasonably substantial sections with interesting shapes and detail such as handles, spouts, lids, hinges, openings, patterns, designs etc. (If there are no appropriate artefacts currently

Photography

in use, consider looking at items such as door and window furniture. You will be surprised how many different forms of handle, lock, closure, hinge or opening device can be found around a school building.) Remind the children to check distances and to make a note of the position of the artefact in the school (if applicable) before taking their photographs.

When the photographs are processed, make enlarged photocopies to show better detail. Let the children cut these up and reassemble them or use them to make patterns or collage pieces arranged in the shape of the original object. Colour can be added to these photocopies with paints, coloured pencils or felt-tipped pens.

If photographs have been taken around the school rather than of specific artefacts they can still be used in the same way or can be displayed to show the range of interesting details around the building. Challenge the rest of the class to try to find exactly where they can be found – thus extending the close observational activity.

Further activities
• Ask the children to record small details of items seen on a walk around the area outside school. The different styles of door furniture, such as letter boxes and door-knockers and gate-fasteners, are fascinating.
• Let the children select ordinary everyday objects and take photographs of only part of them from unusual angles, then ask the other children to identify them. These pictures also can be photocopied and cut so that only small sections are shown. These in turn can be enlarged to make identification more interesting and surprising.
• Undertake the same activity taking photographs of parts of the face, hands, feet or joints.

7. Panorama

Objective
To build a 360° panoramic record.

Age range
Seven to eleven.

Group size
Whole class or small groups.

Time
30 minutes.

What you need
A camera loaded with 36 frame film, spare film, Silva compasses (optional), adhesive, scissors, sheets or strips of card, a measuring tape, examples of the photographic work of David Hockney.

What to do

This activity can be used to follow Activity 5 as the children will need to understand that they are going to turn round slowly through 360° to make a photographic record. However, this activity is going to be rather more precise. Explain that they are going to take a whole series of photographs which they will later join up to form a complete circular representation. Introduce them to the word 'panorama' and explain what it means. Build on any reference points they may have (eg. the BBC television programme of the same name. Does the introduction film footage link in with the name? Is it a good title for a new programme? Why?).

Take the children outside and ask them to select a spot which has an interesting view whichever direction they look. Get the children to test the selection by turning very slowly around and looking carefully at what they can see. Introduce links with mathematics and geography mapping skills by asking the children how many degrees they have turned through. Use references to right angles with younger children or introduce the use of Silva compasses with older children. Develop links with English by asking the children to describe accurately what they can see. Ask them to give reasons why their viewpoint should be the one chosen for the group to use. If necessary, organise a vote!

Ask the children to mark the chosen spot in some way and explain that they will each take a photograph facing outwards, moving the camera only a fraction between shots so that the resulting photographs will show an overlap but that they will be able to be joined together to form a complete circle. Point out that there could be problems ensuring that the photographs are taken from the same height. Ask the children to identify any other potential difficulties and

Photography 101

encourage them to suggest solutions. Show them the measuring tape and see if they can work out suitable ways to check the height (ie. the photographer's eye level) and discuss ways in which this can be kept standard.

A simple solution would be to check the eye level of the smallest pupil and mark the tape at that height, then ask the children to work together to keep the tape taught, checking that each child holds the camera at the right height. Each child could be asked to take one photograph and then remain in position until the next photographer carefully and slowly takes their place, moving only fractionally to take the next shot. This is fairly tricky so make sure the children take enormous care over the changes and do not move the camera away from their finishing position. It might be a good idea to let the children practise this manoeuvre first before taking the photographs so that they understand how precise they have to be.

When they are confident with the process, let each child take a turn to be both the photographer and the assistant and take the photographs. If there are still frames left to take after everyone has had a turn, continue around the 360° a second time, reinforcing the shots. If the film is used up before the panorama is finished, mark the last position very carefully, change the film and complete the process.

When the films are developed, spread all the photographs out on a large table and ask the children to overlap them, carefully building up a complete picture. Discard any that are unnecessary and don't worry if they do not fit squarely next to each other.

At this point, show the children some examples of the photographic work of David Hockney. Encourage the children to discuss it in the light of their own discoveries about photography.

Cut a length of card, or join smaller pieces together, to form a strip longer than the length of the panorama. Mount the photographs on the card strip, then join the ends of the circle to complete the

panorama. This can either be done so that all the photographs are on the inner side of the circle representing the panorama as seen, or the card can be jointed to show the photographs on the outside of the circle giving an alternative view.

Further activities
• The photographs could form a backdrop for models of the school etc.
• The images could be copied to make a print panorama, using polystyrene press print.

8. Child's eye view

Objective
To make a record of everyday things from a different point of view.

Age range
Nine to eleven.

Group size
Small groups.

Time
30 minutes.

What you need
A camera, paper, pencils, card, scissors, adhesive, felt-tipped pens or similar, photocopier.

What to do
This is a good activity to do just before a new intake of young children comes into the school. It is also a good follow-up to the previous activity because it requires children to work at a different height level to their own and needs careful planning.

Explain to the children that their view of school must look very different to that of the very small children starting school for the first time. Ask them if they can remember particular things about starting school. Make a note of anything they can remember that worried them at the time. For instance, lots of small children dread the hustle and bustle of a dinner hall or the great expanse of children at breaktimes. Let the children interview younger children who have been in the school only a year or so to do some real market research.

Next ask the children to work out what is approximately the average height of a new entrant to the school. Discuss how they might find this out. Exploit all the obvious links with mathematics.

Let the children work together to plan out a route commonly used by the new pupils around the school (cloakroom, classroom, hall, toilets, playground etc.) and ask them to take a series of photographs at the new children's eye level. This should give a clear picture of what the young children actually see most of when they arrive at school. Discuss how

this could be done accurately. (You might be quite surprised at the results when the photographs are processed.)

When the children have finished this, ask them to plan out and take the photographs of the times, places and events that are mentioned in the survey where the younger children felt anxious. For example, if children said they were worried about what would happen if they hurt themselves at playtime, the group might want to plan, pose and shoot a photograph of a teacher giving simple first aid to a small child who had a bump in the playground. Similarly, shots of young children being served with lunch, hanging up coats etc. might be appropriate.

When the photographs are processed, either use them for a display or illustration for simple picture-books, with suitable captions added by the children.

Alternatively they could write a story around the pictures. The book could then be used with the new entrants. It might even be possible to photocopy the original book to make individual copies for all the new children coming to school.

9. Photocopy repeats

Objective
To use the same photographic image in a range of ways.

Age range
Five to eleven.

Group size
Whole class in small groups working in pairs.

Time
45 minutes.

What you need
A selection of photographs of objects (preferably taken by the children), large sheets of paper, adhesive, scissors, thin

brushes, watercolour paints or coloured pencils or felt-tipped pens, examples of photographic repeat patterns (eg. Andy Warhol's *Shoes* or *Marilyn Monroe* series), photocopier.

What to do
Collect together a selection of photographs of objects, preferably taken by the children themselves. (Particularly good subjects are shoes, hands, feet, faces, hair, cups and saucers, flowers, schoolbags and canned drinks.) Photocopy each photograph (and enlarge it if possible) about six to eight times.

Show the children the examples of photographs used to make patterns or arranged in a repeat style. Explain how the same base photograph has been used in a different way, or regularly repeated. Discuss how the artist or photographer has chosen the arrangement and ask in what way the photographs have been altered or placed together in a design. Is there any pattern to the arrangement?

Give each child a matching set of photocopies and ask them to arrange them on a sheet of paper. Ask them to consider how many ways they could make a repeat pattern. Remember to stress that the photographs can be turned around or arranged in many different ways. Encourage them to experiment until they find a design that appeals to them. Ask the children to explain the reasons for their choice to their partners and encourage them to ask questions about the other child's arrangement and make positive comment, for example:
• Why did you decide to turn that row upside down?
• I like the shape you have made by using your photograph in that way.

Next get the children to stick the photographs in place. Ask them to look again at the examples and in particular the way the artist has chosen to use small amounts of carefully placed colour. Discuss these choices and any changes that can be seen in the repeated images. Ask the children to think of reasons why colour has been used in this way. Then ask the children to look very carefully at their designs and consider where they could add colour to enhance the effect. Tell them that they can only choose two colours, or two shades of the same colour, and that they can only use it to highlight one area of each photograph. Explain that some areas can be left uncoloured if they wish. When the children have decided on their colours, let them use thin brushes and watercolour paints, coloured pencils or felt-tipped pens to apply colour very precisely and carefully. Stress that the quality of the work is dependent upon delicate colouring. Do not be tempted to allow the use of large brushes and thick pre-mixed paints as these will obliterate the underlying photocopy.

Further activities

- Choose photographs of artefacts linked to a topic theme.
- Use photographs of class members, teachers or staff.
- Restrict the colour highlighting to one colour chosen by the whole class. This could be linked to seasonal colours, such as silver or blue for winter.
- Use the resulting design for printed repeat patterns.

CHAPTER 9

Understanding art and artists

Many teachers are worried about the National Curriculum Art Attainment Target 2, Knowledge and Understanding, because they feel less than confident in their own knowledge of a wide range of artists and their work. This chapter is designed to help teachers overcome these initial feelings of alarm and to offer practical guidance in how to address the issues. An important element to remember is that AT1 should not be taught in isolation but interwoven into the programme of study planned for the children.

Teachers should not be anxious if they do not consider themselves 'artists' or particularly 'artistic'! You do not need to be an acclaimed painter, sculptor or ceramist to be able to help children gain an understanding of how artists work. Nor need you have a detailed knowledge of art history in order to enable children to learn to appreciate the different periods of artistic development and explore the rich array of different ideas expressed through an art medium. There will, in fact, be a real delight and excitement generated in learning alongside the children, seeing old favourite paintings through new eyes as the pupils share their own interpretations, or watching together real artists at work explaining their ideas.

Understanding art and artists 107

BACKGROUND

The National Curriculum Art statutory orders indicate that children should have the experience of seeing artists at work and that they should have opportunities to learn about a range of artistic interpretations. You might well feel at a disadvantage because you do not know of any local artists that you can call upon to work with your school. However, every area has a Regional Arts Board (consult the telephone directory to find a contact point) and each one of these has a range of Arts Officers, usually an Education Officer, who can give you advice. Your local Regional Arts Board may also have a special scheme which offers funding towards particular projects. They will give you full details of any such arrangement and of any particular criteria for making successful bids. They tend to look favourably on requests for funding from new participants seeking to work with local professional artists, but there may be more specific requirements. For example, they may be more favourably disposed towards bids which will have a collaborative strand, eg. between classes, schools or community links. They may also be anxious to promote an equal opportunities policy such as the encouragement of the participation of black artists or the involvement of visually impaired people. Schools can actually use such specifications to bring a context – and reality – to their own school equal opportunity policies! It is essential that you contact your own Regional Arts Board because they all operate individually and may have different funding arrangements and ideas.

However, they should all be able to help supply information about a wide range of local artists and their work, and often the charges they make for schools. For example, if you wanted to contact a sculptor to work with children to produce an exciting three-dimensional construction to go in the entrance hall, your local Regional Arts Board should be able to give you some contacts. Many of them hold data banks of available artists which are a rich source of ideas.

There are also other local sources that may be able to give you assistance. Contact your local library and seek out the names and addresses of any art societies and groups. Usually there will be a club of some form with members who have special talents. Frequently they will be only too pleased to come into school to show children their work and to demonstrate different techniques. It is not necessary for skilled enthusiasts to give formal demonstrations – in fact, this could be pretty daunting for a non-educationalist! There can be a real value in inviting local amateur artists into school and giving them a comfortable space in which to set up a working area. Then as they feel their work is progressing well, you can gently persuade them to let small groups of children come to watch them at work. Inevitably the children will begin to ask questions and if you are sensitively supportive to your visitor – preventing a barrage of over-enthusiastic questions – the artist will soon respond to their interest. It is useful for the children to be able from time to time to see how the work has progressed.

There is also the possibility of leaving ongoing work in a prominent place, such as the hall, so that children have a daily view of the developing study. This can also stimulate the interest of other visitors, parents and governors. This in turn may develop contacts further. Often visitors will know of someone who has a particular talent for other art forms, such as ceramics or embroidery. You may also learn of a contact who has a collection of interesting artefacts, perhaps from another culture or of historical significance, which could form a superb starting point for a range of children's work both in art and other curriculum areas.

If you do decide to use an artist in residence (the correct term for an artist working in school) there are certain points that must be clearly understood by all parties so that the experience is positive and successful. It is vital that everyone's expectations are clear. In general artists are not teachers and cannot be expected to manage a class or group of children. Obviously a teacher must be in charge of the class or group at any particular time. Artists may not be familiar with the sort of routines teachers live with (sessions times, clearing up, class ground rules etc.) and you will need to ensure they understand these and are not taken unawares by sudden demands on their time – or patience!

It is also essential that definite arrangements concerning the role of the

Understanding art and artists **109**

artist, the time commitment, the size of groups, the available materials, the size and arrangement of working space, specific desired outcomes of the residency (eg. wall-hanging, pottery ready for firing etc.) and charges where applicable are known and agreed. A letter addressing all these issues and others particular to the school should be sent and signed confirmations received before the visit. This will not only form a very simple contract, but more importantly, a shared awareness of the purpose and practicalities of the venture. Usually residencies proceed very smoothly and everybody benefits greatly but it can be very frustrating and spoil otherwise successful links when each party thinks the other one is responsible for tidying up and clearing away! Don't get too despondent if your artist only wants to work with small groups. Enlist the help of parents to help keep the ratios in balance. If supervision by a teacher is a problem, consider using the school hall so that a teacher is present in the area to keep an overall eye on things whilst the artist works in one corner. Always go for a quality experience. It is much better to concentrate work with a small group for a lengthy period of time than to 'process' great numbers of children during a frantic day. Because the process is the valuable part of the experience, be sure to have a camera or video ready to record the workshop. Let the children take turns to record parts of the experience which they feel are important. Then they can each make a presentation to the rest of the group which can extend the range and quality of the learning quite considerably.

Another rich source of artist's work can be local colleges. An approach to their art departments can often yield examples of student's work on loan. This work can be very interesting as it often illustrates a varied range of styles and approaches as part of the course work. Sometimes the work will include very large pieces of sculpture and paintings which can be exciting for small children to investigate. Often the students are happy to come along and talk about their ideas and how they have chosen to interpret them. If you are really lucky you might get a college to

provide you with a rolling programme of exhibits to enrich your school!

Another source of expertise will undoubtedly be your nearest art gallery. Most galleries will have an education officer, or someone who will liaise with teachers. Some of the larger galleries have loan services and can arrange to let schools have drawings, paintings etc. for a specific period.

There is enormous benefit in making a class visit to a gallery. For many children this may be the very first visit they have made and so care must be taken to ensure that it is a magical experience. You will need to make a pre-visit yourself to discuss the possibilities with the education officer personally. He or she will readily suggest appropriate exhibits for a planned visit, which can often be linked to a particular period of history being studied (eg. Tudors and Victorians). Alternatively the visit could possibly follow a special theme, such as family life, towns, seasons etc. A different approach might be to compare the work of two of three very different artists.

The gallery will probably be able to arrange a special guided tour of the chosen exhibits which will teach children how to read works of art and give a great deal of background information about the artists and their life and times. Most galleries welcome children and are happy to let them work with sketch books around the building. Some provide areas for eating packed lunches, together with special storage areas for the usual personal clutter children cart about with them. Larger galleries usually have a good shop where children can buy quality postcards, booklets etc.

A visit to a gallery provides a great impetus to understanding art and artists and makes an excellent basis for a whole-class visit with accompanying parents. In some cases the education officers will come to your school and bring information and exhibits. Contact your nearest gallery for a schedule of the year's forthcoming exhibitions and attractions. There is an ever-increasing number of events which are specially designed for children. Many galleries also have artists in residence and can arrange practical workshops for children.

Understanding art and artists 111

ACTIVITIES

1. Everyday objects

Objective
To encourage careful observation of artists' work.

Age range
Five to eleven.

Group size
Whole class or groups.

Time
At least one hour.

What you need
A timeline, reproductions of several contrasting paintings depicting chairs, furniture or household objects (such as Van Gogh's bedroom at Arles or his chair paintings; the Dutch masters' interior paintings are good examples but any paintings of contrasting styles will do), a chair or another item of everyday furniture, drawing and painting materials, chalkboard or large sheet of paper.

What to do
Show the children the first painting and ask them to describe what they see in the picture. They will probably list the objects depicted. Then ask them to look at the colours the artist has used:
• Are they bright or more sombre?
• Are there strong contrasts or close shades?
• What was the weather like on the day the picture was painted?
• What time of day do the colours suggest?
• Is there a light source? If so what is it?
• Which direction is it coming from?

Write down the most interesting comments on the board or on a large sheet of paper for later reference by the children.

Ask the children to look at the way the artist has used the paint (or pastel etc.) to depict the objects.
• Are they drawn boldly using thick paint or very finely with tiny brushstrokes?
• Do they have clear outlines or are they made up of broken sections of colour?
• How thick do they think the paint is on the real painting?
• Why did the artist choose to

112 Chapter 9

use paint in this way?
• What do they imagine the artist was thinking about when he or she decided to paint this particular scene?

Write down helpful suggestions from the children's responses.

Now get them to consider the artist wanted the person looking at the painting to feel. You might be surprised at the ideas the children will give you. They can be very imaginative and are not as inhibited about artworks as adults often can be! Ask them to decide whether the artist painted the picture from their experience, imagination or from direct observation.

Make a point of asking the children whether the painting was done recently or a long time ago. Ask them to look for clues in the picture before answering. What evidence do they have for their guess? Discuss their ideas and then put a marker on a timeline to show them the correct historical reference point. Briefly link this with any major event that the children may be familiar with, for instance, Victorian times in Britain or voyages of discovery.

Put the first painting on display and produce a contrasting work. Repeat the discussion process using this new stimulus, writing down the children's ideas on a second list. Do not rush this activity – sufficient time spent now will greatly enrich children's understanding. There are obviously excellent opportunities to extend English work.

Next ask the children to decide in what ways the paintings are similar and dissimilar.

Finally place a chair or some other suitable item of furniture in a prominent place. Ask the children to choose one of the artists they have looked at and to paint a picture of the chair using the same style. Ask them to refer to the original painting and the list of comments constantly to check they are adopting the same styles. This may seem a difficult task but you will be amazed how well children, even quite young children, can absorb the flavour of artists' styles and reproduce this essence in their own work.

Further activities

• Ask the children to paint or draw a picture of a corner of their own bedroom or a piece of favourite furniture at home.
• Repeat the activity selecting works that depict flowers. There is such a huge range of works to choose from that it should be possible to select paintings that span a considerable historical period. Moreover, there will be a great variety of styles and media to compare, for example oils, watercolours, collage, pastels and prints.
• Follow the same activity looking at animals in a range of paintings (for example, in the works of Rousseau, Dürer, Dali etc.).

Understanding art and artists

2. Staffroom mugs

Objective
To develop observation and inquiry into ceramics.

Age range
Seven to eleven.

Group size
Whole class or small groups.

Time
One hour.

What you need
A collection of staff cups and mugs (or if these are by some miracle matching, a collection of different ceramic drinking utensils!), a table, chalkboard or large sheet of paper, pencils, small sheets of paper (A5), a jug of water, a measuring jug or cylinder.

What to do
Arrange the collection of cups and mugs on the table and ask the children to look closely at them. Ask one or two children to choose the ones that appeal to them the most. Let them pick up their chosen ones and describe them in detail to the other children. Help them by prompting with questions designed to make them concentrate on the item. Ask whether the mug is handmade or mass produced. How can they tell? You may need to introduce the idea of individually made pots and ask them to look for the evidence of this. Ask them to look for any makers' marks on the base. Are there any words on the base? What colour clay is it made from? Hold it up to the light and test whether it is opaque or translucent. (You may need to talk about bone china and stoneware).

Write down a list of points to consider on the board or on a sheet of paper. These should include the following questions:
• Does it have a pattern?
• Is there any decoration?
• Is it hand-painted or decorated by transfer?
• Is it raised or flat? If it is raised or indented, how is it made? Can you see any of the potter's 'rings' where the fingers have raised and shaped the clay (usually on the inside)? Can you see where it has been cut off the wheel or has it a 'turned' foot?
• How many colours have been used?
• How have the colours been applied?
• Does it have a rim decoration? Is this hand-painted? How has the maker kept it even?
• How is the handle fixed on?
• If a cup and saucer has been chosen, how do these match?

Then ask the children to consider the shape, size and feel of the mug or cup. Is it comfortable to hold? Would it still be comfortable with a hot drink in it? How much liquid does it hold? (You can make some good mathematical links here by asking children to arrange the mugs in order of capacity and then by testing their guesses with water and a measuring jug.)

You may even be able to consider the age of the mug, or ascertain if it was made for a special occasion (for example commemorative mugs, club fund-raisers etc.). You might also consider the cost of buying the different types of mug. Next ask a child to choose one of the mugs or cups and, without directly pointing it out, describe it only using the range of questions already used. Encourage the others to try to identify if from the general description. You can repeat this once or twice. When there has been sufficient discussion to enable the children to understand the questions to ask about each mug, ask each child or very small groups of children (depending on resources) to draw their chosen item carefully on a piece of A5 paper and add a written description. They can also carefully measure the capacity of their mug and add this information to their visual record.

When all the records are completed there should be a fairly substantial body of knowledge about pottery accumulated just from the staffroom equipment!

Further activities

• Bring in a collection of mugs and cups that are from other countries or cultures (such as oriental tea bowls, French coffee bowls etc.) Let the chidren investigate into the different materials and styles that are used, and the customs surrounding their use. Why do these vary?

• Include older examples which illustrate designs from earlier times. You can probably find these by asking around friends and colleagues. Better still, ask the children and their parents to bring any interesting specimens to school. You might even be lucky enough to find a visitor who is a collector and who will talk about their collection.
• Arrange for a potter or ceramist to visit school to talk about their work.
• Look at examples and prices in catalogues. Write to manufacturers to enquire how their products are made.
• Study illustrations in history books to look for different shapes and types of drinking vessel. Find out how they were made.
• Ask the children to design their own drinking vessels for a particular purpose or purposes, such as for tea with important visitors or mugs for a party or picnic.

Understanding art and artists

3. Telling the story

Objective
To encourage children to look for detail and symbolism in paintings.

Age range
Five to eleven.

Group size
Whole class or smaller groups.

Time
45 minutes.

What you need
A large sized print of a painting (appropriate to the children's age range) depicting a scene including figures. (Good examples might be: Renaissance religious paintings; Gericault *Raft of the Medusa*; Bruegel *Hunters in the Snow*; Pre-Raphaelite work such as Millais *Widow's Mite*; Seurat *Bathers at Asnières*; Munch *Angst*; Degas *Absinthe Drinker*; Beryl Cook *Breakfast Time*).

What to do
Organise the room so that the children can see the picture clearly. Ask the children to look very carefully at the picture for two minutes without talking and to try to work out from all the clues in the painting what appears to be happening. Then let several children give their opinions and discuss these for a few minutes, asking the children to show what parts of the painting give them their ideas. If the children find this difficult draw their attention to some of the smaller details which give some possible indications of an unfolding story.

Next let the children look at the particular characters in the picture. Ask them to look at the clothes and decide whether the people are rich or poor, why they are dressed in a particular manner (eg. for their work, for a celebration etc.), what colours they are wearing, what sort of fabric their clothes are made from, and what historical time they live in. You may need to explain that artists often paint famous events from times earlier than their own.

Now suggest that they consider what each figure is doing, has just done or is perhaps about to do. Ask them to look particularly at the position of the limbs. Then ask them to look at the expressions on each character's face and to decide what each one is thinking. Are they happy, sad, frightened, angry, relaxed? Look together to see if there are any clues in the painting to help you decide.

Then ask for volunteers to pretend to be the characters in the painting. Let these children come to the front and imitate the position of the

figures they have chosen to represent. Ask each child in turn to pretend to be their character and to speak their thoughts aloud. If the children are confident enough, ask them to have a short conversation together in character. Encourage the rest of the class to ask these characters questions. You may need to take a lead briefly. Good leading questions would be:
- What work do you do?
- Where do you live?
- Do you have any family?
- Why do you look so worried?

If you are working with the whole class divide the children into groups and ask each group to act out a short scene, only one minute long, to show what happened immediately before the moment depicted in the painting. Let each group demonstrate their ideas and suggest the other children ask them questions.

When the drama activity has been fully explored, bring the children back to observe the painting. Now ask the children to think why the artist painted the picture and what he or she wanted the observer to think or feel about the characters and the scene. Explain that there is no absolutely right answer but that everyone looking at a painting can have an acceptable point of view. However, a little research can often result in information about the artist's own ideas.

Further activities
- Cut out large balloon shapes and ask the children to write words in these, attributing them to particular characters. Arrange them on a display around the painting.
- Make a class book explaining the story behind the painting, written from the point of view of the characters.
- Choose a painting with an animal in it. Ask the children to tell the story the animal would relate if it could speak.
- Find out some information about the artist and the time in which he or she lived to display beside the children's ideas about the painting.
- Choose paintings on the same theme and compare ideas. If possible, choose paintings from different periods. (For example, it would be interesting to compare the ways in which Giotto, El Greco and Dali depicted the Crucifixion.)

Understanding art and artists

4. Mystery and imagination

Objective
To explore imaginative representations in painting.

Age range
Seven to eleven.

Group size
Whole class or small groups.

Time
One hour.

What you need
Large prints of surrealistic or symbolic paintings (good examples would be the surrealistic paintings by Hieronymus Bosch, William Blake or Salvador Dali), card frames, paper for each child, painting and drawing materials.

What you do
Select a painting that you think will be suitable to promote real interest. Set this up in an area where all the children can see it clearly. If you have chosen paintings which are very complex and 'busy', such as those by Hieronymus Bosch, it would be useful to make a small frame out of card so that you can isolate specific zones to be observed.

Explain that these paintings have been created by the artists to represent particular ideas they wished to express. It might be useful to use the idea of dreaming as an example to explain the initial strangeness of their work. Tell the children to think of dreams they have had where everything was rather magical and different to real life, but where things all seemed to be fairly acceptable in the context of the dream. Often dreams, although weird, can be enormous fun. Sometimes of course, they can be terrifying nightmares. Now ask the children to look at the paintings as if they represent the artist's dream. Try to discover how large the original work is so that children can have an idea of the actual size as reproductions can be very misleading.

Now ask the children to look at the overall picture. Is it of one subject or of many things? Do the different things seem to be related or are they different? Are things painted in fine detail or more loosely and vaguely? How are they arranged in the painting? Are they separate or do they intertwine? What are the predominant colours? How does the painting make the children feel? Is it funny? Frightening? Odd? Interesting? Are there any familiar things which appear in an unusual way?

If the picture is very 'busy', use the card frame to isolate sections of the painting and ask the children to look carefully at these. (Be aware that you might find some rum 'goings-on' in some of Hieronymus Bosch's work and be prepared for this. You

118 *Chapter 9*

might wish to be selective!) Discuss how some film-makers, such as Steven Spielberg, often try to weave a dreamlike quality into their films, using special effects. Explain that a painter is restricted to two-dimensional limits and has to try to make an impact through the way he or she depicts things on a flat surface. Stress that these artists wanted the observers to feel differently about their work. They wanted to challenge people to see things in a different way to normal. Now ask the children to think of a dream they may have had – or invent one – where normal everyday objects somehow became very different, or where very unusual things happened because familiar things had been changed in some way. Discuss these ideas and, if necessary, give some absurd examples to stimulate thought. For example, you might talk about an armchair made entirely of water or a car covered with mirrors etc.

Ask the children to choose an everyday object and paint it in a totally new way, to try to show a dream quality.

Further activities
• When the individual paintings are completed, use them to make a collage to illustrate a surrealistic dream world.
• Look at some of the other work of Dali, including his three-dimensional structures, such as the lobster telephone.
• Blake's works were often engravings. Look at how he used carefully drawn lines to convey his ideas. Ask the children to create strange creatures using finely drawn lines, adding colour afterwards with a thin brush. Look at how his engravings were used as illustrations.
• Look at the imaginative work of Miró, in particular his painting *Harlequin's Carnival*. The work of Magritte is also strange and exciting, challenging the imagination and providing an excellent stimulus for children.
• Create three-dimensional representations from surprising materials, using soft fabrics to make normally rigid items and vice versa (soft bookshelves, wooden cakes etc.).
• Use colour magazines and cut out everyday items to make collages where the items have been mixed up into a sort of dream world, such as a kitchen scene full of large insects and gardening tools or a family of budgies in a sitting room with a cage full of people.

Understanding art and artists

5. Using the local church

Objective
To look at craftsmanship in a local setting.

Age range
Five to eleven.

Group size
Whole class, working in small groups.

Time
Half a day.

What you need
Sketch books, drawing pencils, large sheets of paper, large wax crayons, drafting tape, camera.

What to do
Before the activity, establish contact with the local church and find out a little about the history of the building. If the building is very old you are exceptionally lucky because you will have a superb resource for looking at a real range of crafts over a considerable period of time. However, even younger buildings can be a rich source of information and stimulus. Consider the following activities, all of which can be later followed by the children working in small groups. Look first at the site of the church. If there is a graveyard attached, look at the gravestones and try to find examples made of different types of stone. These often vary from district to district. For example, you can see a lot of black polished slate headstones around the Welsh borders.

Look at the inscriptions and the way they are carved. Look at the styles of lettering and try to find the dates for them. Try to discover when it became fashionable to inset letters on to the stones rather than carving them. How is this done? Are there any sculptor's identification marks or initials? Show the children how to tape a large sheet of paper over an interesting headstone and rub over the carving with firm movements using the side of a large wax crayon. Explain that they should press fairly hard but be careful to avoid ripping the paper.

120 Chapter 9

Look at the other decorative carving. Can you find a range of styles and give dates? Look at those which are line carvings and those which are in relief, standing out from the stone. Ask the children to feel them and try to discover the grooves and cuts made by the carving tools. Make a record of the different styles of grave and tombs, for example those with table-tops or flat with kerbstones.

Now walk around the building. Look up frequently and look out for decorative carving and patterns on the stones. Can you see how stones have been shaped to fit together? Are tool marks evident? Are there any areas where the stonework has decayed? Does this help you see how the building was constructed?

Look particularly at the windows. Sketch the shapes of the various windows, noting especially the places where the stone has been worked into different shapes. Ask the children to decide how this was done and how many pieces of stone were used. Are there any decorative gargoyles or drain spouts? Make a record of them and discover how old they are.

Look at the roof and steeple or tower, if there is one. Are there any special tile patterns? What is the roof made from? How large are the slates or tiles? What is the guttering made from? Are there any special decorations on it?

Now look at the doors and entrances. Can you see any sculptures around them? If there are any figures, encourage the children to make drawings of them to identify later. (Note particularly what any figures might be holding in their hands – these give valuable clues). Are there any patterns around the doorway? If there are any low enough, let the children tape a large sheet of paper over the stone and gently but firmly rub it with

Understanding art and artists 121

the wax crayons, always rubbing in the same direction if possible. Ask the children to try to feel the sculptor's marks.

Remember to look at the door itself. What is it made of? Can you see how the pieces fit together? What sort of nails or joints have been used? Ask the group to make a sketch of the 'door furniture' – locks, bolts, hinges etc. Is there any special decorative work evident on the metal? Look at the inside of the door as well as the outside! How does it fasten into the wall?

Inside the building look at the windows and any stained glass. Which is the oldest glass? Is there any story depicted? If so, which story is it? Explain to the children that in older churches the stained glass served as a picture book of Bible stories to help the majority of poor folk who could not read. Which colour predominates? Take particular note of how the faces are depicted and also how the sections of glass are joined together. Photograph sections for later examination.

In younger buildings, look at the style of any stained glass designs. In what way are they different to older styles? Are the segments fastened together in any different ways? Are the colours different? Is the glass itself smooth or ridged and bubbled? Are there any dates or craftsmen's names?

Find out about the church furniture. Look at the pews, the pulpit, the font and the lectern. What materials are they made from? Notice particularly any carving and let the group make drawings of it, or make rubbings if this is possible. Look carefully for any original elements. For instance, 'Mousie' Thompson, a brilliant woodcarver and designer, always carved at least one mouse on his work. Explore the choir stalls and priests' seats. There might be a Bishop's throne if your local church is a big one. Often these are heavily embellished with woodcarving of high quality. Encourage the children to feel the shapes and designs in the wood and to look out for any items in wrought iron. Often there are candle-holders or light-fittings and sometimes screens and rails.

Be sure to look closely at the structure of the nave. Examine the supporting pillars, the way they join the roof, any vaulting and any carving or special features. Often there is evidence of wall

122 Chapter 9

painting and decoration. Hopefully you will have made special arrangements with someone from the church who can show you the church plate – the chalices, patens, candlesticks and other religious artefacts that belong to that particular church. These can often be very old and it will be a wonderful experience for children to witness at first hand crafted items of high quality and beauty. Again, visual records should be made.

Finally, look at fabric and thread work. Often you will be able to see the vestments and see how these religious garments are made and decorated. Sometimes churches have very old examples with intricate embroidery and thread work but modern designs are also very interesting and will show children skilled craftswork in context. There may also be hangings and other sewn items in church, including tapestry 'kneelers' and altar frontals.

Also remember to look down and study medieval floor tiles which often feature interlacing designs made with different coloured clays. There can be an enormous range of different craftwork in and around one building. Moreover, there can be opportunities to handle work created by artists and designers hundreds of years ago!

On their return to school, the children can produce a significant record of their study for display and discussion. This can naturally form a good link with a local history study, RE and technology.

Further activities
• Make similar visits to a temple, mosque or synagogue, but remember that some artefacts may not be generally handled. Be sensitive to other cultures.
• Children can make tapestry squares. These can be kept as individual work or combined to make a class wall-hanging, screen, cover for the back of an upright piano etc.
• Children can experiment with carving into blocks or tiles of clay to investigate different effects using different tools. (Remember solid blocks of clay cannot be safely fired.)
• Give children small blocks of balsa wood to carve into shapes seen on the visit.
• Older children can paint on classroom windows, using poster paint or paint mixed with PVA medium, to experiment with 'stained glass' effects.

Understanding art and artists

6. Posters

Objective
To look at design and graphics used in a range of posters.

Age range
Seven to eleven.

Group size
Whole class, working in pairs.

Time
One hour.

What you need
A selection of posters including examples of work by Toulouse-Lautrec and Alphonse Mucha, small sheets of paper (A5), large sheets of paper (A3), drawing pencils, a selection of watercolour brushes, water pots, palettes, watercolour paints (tempera, gouache or powder), old toothbrushes, mixing trays, a timeline, scissors, paper adhesive.

What to do
This is a very good activity to do when there is a real need for posters to advertise a school or community event. You can then put the children in the same position as artists who receive a commission for similar work! They will need to work to a deadline, convey particular information and plan out high-impact visual designs.

Ask the children to bring in any posters they can – or search through colour supplements for suitable materials. Try to obtain posters advertising local events (approach your local council leisure services, information services or library) and display these for the children to study. Encourage the children to make critical judgements of these. Ask them if each poster fulfils its purpose:
• Does it give sufficient or too much information?
• Does it attract the eye so people want to read it?
• Is the colour choice attractive and appropriate?
• Is it memorable or rather boring?
• Is the lettering well chosen?

Now put these posters to one side and explain that you are going to look together at the work of some artists who also designed posters. Tell the children the periods in which your chosen artist lived, marking the appropriate dates on the timeline and drawing the children's attention to other events around the same period.

Now display some of the artists' posters, one by one, asking the children to make the same critical analysis of these as they did with the earlier posters. Encourage the children to discuss each one in detail. Explain that these posters were created by artists, not just printers, and that they spent many hours making sketches and preparatory drawings before producing the final designs. Ask them to look particularly at the way in which colour is used. Is it used in blocks of straight colour, or is it shaded? Or do the colours change gradually? How many different colours have been used? Are there any colours which overlap? Are there any special effects created? (Point out Toulouse-Lautrec's technique called *crachis*, or 'spitting'. This was produced by splattering ink from a toothbrush to create a speckled effect.)

Ask the children to look at the distinctive style of each artist. Look at the way Mucha uses flowers and foliage in his work, and his use of pattern and curving lines. Compare this with the way Toulouse-Lautrec favours huge blocks of colour and very strong lines. (He was influenced by oriental artists and their use of flat colour.) Explain that both artists did many sketches and then selected from these to plan out the poster.

Now ask the children to work in pairs to prepare their own posters advertising a special school event or something similar. Ask them to choose the style of one of the artists they have seen and to try to plan out their poster in the same way. By working in

Understanding art and artists 125

pairs the children can use each other as models for their sketches where necessary. For example, for a concert they might wish to depict someone singing, playing an instrument or dancing. (However, each child will eventually produce their own poster.) Ask them to work fairly quickly, sketching on the smaller sheets of paper and preparing several different sketches from which they can make a final selection.

Ask the children to decide what information should appear on the posters and write this clearly on the board as a reference for later. When the preparation sketches are done, let the pairs discuss together which drawings each will select and how they will develop them in the same sort of styles as their chosen artist. When each child has decided, ask them to enlarge their sketch by drawing it on the A3 paper, considering carefully where they will position it. Ask them whether it will be more effective in the centre, to one side or nearer the top or bottom. Or could they put several different sketches together to produce a busier scene? Make sure they constantly refer back to the examples.

Next ask the children to consider the lettering. How will it fit around the sketches? Ask them to refer back to the original posters for ideas and letter shapes. Now let the children experiment on the small sheets of paper with possible letter forms. Ask the pairs to discuss together and help each other choose the style and size of the letters.

These can be drawn and cut out so that the children can arrange them on their posters before choosing the final position. When the final place has been decided, show them how to use the cut-outs as templates and lightly draw round the shapes. (It is also possible to stick the letters on later if this is preferred). When all the preliminary drafting has been done, the children can begin to paint their posters, referring to the original posters to check style. If they want to use the *crachis* method, tell them to follow this procedure.

126 | Chapter 9

- Mix up a fairly thin dark paint in a mixing tray.
- Screen off with paper all the areas which are not to be splattered.
- Ensure that no one or nothing valuable is in the line of fire.
- Dip the old toothbrush into the paint.
- Hold the toothbrush close to the chosen area and pull your finger across the tufts towards yourself, so the splatters fall on to the paper.
- Leave the paint to dry before removing the paper screens. This will help to prevent possible smudging.

When all the posters are completed, display them where they can be seen by the children: the corridor is a good place if traffic permits. Let the children look at each poster in turn and analyse them in the same way as they studied the originals. Naturally, the finished posters should be displayed around the school or neighbourhood to advertise your function and the children's talent!

7. People

Objective
To look at the way different artists depict the human figure.

Age range
Five to eleven.

Group size
Whole class working in pairs or small groups.

Time
One hour.

What you need
A collection of postcards and art books showing different paintings of people (Choose contrasting styles. Good suggestions would be: Beryl Cook – chubby folk; El Greco – thin figures; Lowry – matchstick folk; Holman Hunt – detailed), paper and drawing pencils, a large print of a figure painting/drawing, chalkboard or large sheet of paper, large paper clips.

What to do
Tell the children that artists can choose to show their ideas through the way they choose to paint. Explain that you are

Understanding art and artists 127

going to look at the way some artists have chosen to portray people and that you have chosen a selection of different styles.

Show the class your large print. Ask the children if they can decide what the mood of the painting is. Are the figures happy, sad, angry or relaxed, or is there some other general feeling from the picture?

Now ask them to look at the way the artist has painted the figures. Are they large or small, lean or hefty? Encourage children to use as wide a range of adjectives as possible. Make a note of these words on the board or on a separate sheet of paper as these can be useful to develop into written work later.

Ask the children to look at the positions of the bodies of the people in the picture. Are they bent over, spread widely or tightly compact? Do they dominate the picture or are they only a small part of the available space? Is all the figure shown or only part of it? Get the children to think why the artist has chosen to show them in this way and place them in the picture in a certain place.

Draw out the idea that people show their feelings in their movements as well as in their faces. Discuss the reasons for the artist choosing this particular composition. Does putting a figure towards the edge of a painting instead of the centre make any difference to the way observers think about it? Does it convey any particular feeling? Gather the opinions of the children. Suggest that drawing only part of a figure or placing it in an unusual part of the painting can make the viewer look at it very differently.

Although the colours each artist has chosen will be important and carefully selected, the aim of this activity is not to analyse their use of colour so much as to consider the way in which the figures have been drawn. Accept comments on the use of colour but highlight the other aspects of the figure. Ask the children to work in pairs or small groups and distribute the postcards or art books. If you are using books, use paper clips to hold the pages open at the appropriate place. Next ask the pairs or groups to look at the prints for five minutes and discuss them, thinking of comments that they can share with the class.

Explain that everyone is to have at least one comment ready. Give them time to do this whilst you circulate and 'eavesdrop'.

Spend a few minutes sharing these comments after each group has briefly described their picture. Then ask the children to try to imagine what the chosen figure(s) would do next. Ask them to draw their figure in this new situation, using only pencil and working in the same style as the artist.

As the drawings are completed, ask the children to show the rest of the group both their original picture and their imagined follow-up. Get them to write a few words or sentences – according to their age – to explain their ideas. With young children the teacher can act as scribe.

Further activities
• Get the children to draw themselves or each other in the same style.
• Paint or draw animals using the same styles.

• Prepare very large, almost life-size, paintings of the chosen figures and display them prominently together. Add the children's explanations, plus any stories and poems about their characters. This can make a very dramatic display for a hall or entrance area and be a focus for extending art education throughout the school.

8. Rooms of character

Objective
To study the individual characteristics of artists.

Age range
Nine to eleven.

Group size
Pairs or small groups.

Time
At least two hours.

What you need
A cardboard box for each group (shoebox size), card, coloured paper, adhesive, scraps of fabric, scissors, paints, brushes, mixing trays, modelling materials, a range of art books, posters, postcards etc.

What to do
Decide whether you wish to explore the life and work of a few specific artists or a wide range. This may, in fact, be determined by the range of reference resources that you have available, but this activity could be planned in advance and a collection could be borrowed from the library

Understanding art and artists

service, or from within the school resources by prior arrangement. This can be linked in well with previous work undertaken from earlier activities in this book or form developments of other classwork, linking in with a historical study for instance.

First of all talk to the children about the life and work of an artist you particularly find interesting. It is better if you can refer back to an artist that the children have encountered in some of the other activities in this chapter so they feel a little familiar with the process of looking at an artist's style. Ask them to look at the strong characteristics of their work. For example, Beryl Cook's paintings always depict very plump figures dressed in bright colours; Van Gogh loved the use of raw yellows and blues and worked with very thick paint; Henry Moore's sculptures feature sweeping shapes with holes through them etc.

Now ask them to consider what sort of a room the artist would have lived in which would show some elements of his or her life and style of working – a sort of fantasy room! Ask the children to think about the artists you have discussed with them and try to identify the design of their rooms. For instance, what would be in a Beryl Cook room? Perhaps it would have large, chubby furniture. Ask them what this might be like. Would it be made of wood or softer upholstery? What sort of fabrics would she have for the coverings, for curtains and for wallpaper? What colours would she have probably chosen judging from the colours she liked to use in her paintings? What kinds of ornaments and personal things would you see in the room? What paintings

130 Chapter 9

would she have on the wall? What evidence of her personal interests, life-style and family might there be in the room? Draw out of these discussions the need to do some research about the artist in order to fill in the details. You will need to consider when the artists lived, where they lived, whether they did other jobs besides being an artist, whether they had a family etc. If a child asks you a question you cannot answer, use it as an opportunity to say that you will need to find out! Repeat the exercise with at least one other artist so that you can highlight the individual differences that make them unique.

Now tell the children that they are going to create their own rooms for one special artist. You may decide which artists to investigate or give the children a free choice. You can restrict the choice to a particular period (such as the Victorians), or a country, or a type of artist (such as Surrealists) to link in with specific work. Tell them that when their rooms are complete they will display them and explain to the rest of the class why they have decided on their special design.

Distribute the art books and resources and ask the children to work in pairs or small groups. Explain that they first need to research all they can under several headings – write these up somewhere to remind the children. Draw the ideas for headings from your earlier discussions with the class. Remind them that the time an artist lives is significant and that they should look at some of the important events that happened during their lifetimes that might have influenced them, not just personal events but also national and international happenings.

Suggest that they look at a whole range of the artists' work, including different art forms. Draw their attention to the fact that many artists change their styles over a period of time as they develop new ideas (Picasso is an excellent example) and that their rooms can reflect this. Alternatively they could choose just one particular period that appeals to them. Ask them to make notes together in their groups or pairs before they start building their design. Circulate around the groups as they plan and research to check and challenge their notes and

Understanding art and artists

ideas. Again, do not worry if there are facts you do not know or understand about any artist – enjoy the chance to investigate and discover alongside the children! It is a very powerful learning experience for a child to teach you something new!

When you feel the group has a sufficient basis to work from, let them look at available materials and select appropriate items to create their rooms. Probably they will need to paint their own wallpaper designs, prepare tiny paintings for the wall or fashion small artefacts (Van Gogh's pipe perhaps!). Some groups may want to cut away one side of their box to make a sort of stage set, others may want to keep the whole box intact. This process can take some time but the group's bits and pieces can be placed inside their box and stored neatly between sessions.

As the rooms are finished, time should be allowed for the designers to explain their choice of design and to answer questions from the rest of the class. They can also prepare short written texts to accompany their models and add to the display.

Further activities
- Design hats for the chosen artists.
- Design a suitable birthday card for the chosen artist, reflecting their interests, for example a card with holes in for Henry Moore.
- Make a cup and saucer based on the same idea.
- Look at the work of Monet and his wonderful garden at Giverney, then create an artist's dream garden.
- Build the artist's fantasy home.

CHAPTER 10

Developing the school environment

It is possible to enhance the school environment, both interior and exterior, in a way that not only adds to the aesthetic quality of the surroundings but also provides an invaluable resource for art and other areas of the curriculum. The developments can be extremely cost-effective and flexible. They could comprise a series of small projects that would improve the learning environment over a period of time. For example, individual classes could be asked to promote special developments, or the whole school, different year groups or phases could be allowed to take responsibility for an overall plan.

Although each project can specifically enrich the children's understanding of art and give contextual opportunities for practical work and the acquisition of skills, the links with other areas of the curriculum can also be well forged. For example, a project to plan, design and create an 'art garden' would have very obvious links with the National Curriculum for Geography (Geographical Skills, Thematic Study).

Developing the school environment   133

BACKGROUND

Creating a room or area within the school representing the art, crafts and design of a particular period in history would give a real opportunity for children to develop both artistic skills and a deeper understanding of the period chosen for study. The children could even be given the chance to study artefacts from earlier times and civilisations and to use these to search for evidence in exactly the same way as the archaeologist or historian seeks to read the 'clues' of the past. There could be a Viking area, or a Tudor corridor, a Greek mural, and classes could be asked to provide resources from their own work.

Because any project of this kind will need careful planning, research, investigation and building, there are obvious links with technology. It is virtually impossible to undertake such an environmental project without utilising technological process skills and teachers could capitalise on these natural curriculum links.

Displaying children's work

All schools are used to displaying work in classrooms and around the school. Often these displays are temporary with a limited life-span. However, with some thought and minimal outlay the quality of some of these can be improved considerably and the materials used for a greatly extended period of time.

Relatively cheap 'clip together' picture frames can be purchased from DIY stores. These come in many sizes but the largest A3 size is the most useful. These are easy to use as children's paintings, drawings, designs, plans and sketches can be swiftly

mounted and slipped into the frame. In this way, with the purchase of just a few frames, work can be regularly changed with very little effort. The removed work can be easily stored in flat A1 portfolios for later display elsewhere. These portfolios can be bought from cut-price stationery shops at reasonable prices or can be made from packing cases. Ask your local electrical shops or departmental stores for their old packing cases. Refrigerator and washing-machine boxes are perfect. Simply cut down the two longest opposite sides, cut off superfluous end flaps and you have two large portfolios.

Displaying resources

An important element in enhancing the school environment is the resources which are available for use by teachers both in classrooms and in stimulating displays. Many schools will have a selection of framed prints of well-known paintings – often as a result of the initial allocation by an LEA when the school opened. Often these have been hanging in corridors or in odd rooms, gathering dust and rarely looked at, if at all. Sometimes these can be a valuable resource but if they are badly faded, damaged or of poor quality, discard the print itself and use the frame for something more exciting and useful. (Activity 1 in this chapter offers a range of ideas to help you to build up a really dynamic collection.) Consider also adding interesting photographs and posters to the collection. These, along with special newspapers and magazines can form an important part of historical resources for investigation.

In addition to prints, children need to see a whole range of different art forms and styles at first hand. Gradually a collection of drawings, watercolour paintings, work in acrylic, oils or mixed media can be amassed. Obviously no school will be able to afford to outlay huge sums of money, but it is quite possible to supplement examples of the children's own work with a few inexpensive purchases. Often colleges will have similar exhibitions of students' work where individual pieces could be bought. Similarly local art societies and craft fairs can offer a few reasonably priced treasures. It is a good idea to ask the staff to agree to earmark a definite amount of money each year – and account for this in the school's annual financial planning – to

Developing the school environment 135

buy perhaps one or two art works of real quality. The school's PTA may also help in this way, particularly if they can be involved alongside the children in the choices. In a few years the school will have a unique collection which will probably accrue in value.

Occasionally good examples of hand-crafted pottery can be discovered at car boot sales or on 'white elephant' stalls, as can pieces of interesting weaving (for example, bags and wall hangings) brought back from holiday and now no longer required. It is also possible to find interesting fabrics to use as drapes but do make sure that they are clean and suitable. Old curtains are only of value if they are made of particularly good unfaded fabric. Make sure that they look effective once the curtain headings have been removed. This is essential; nothing looks worse than old curtains on otherwise elegant displays. Be careful if you are going to buy prints and paintings at second-hand stalls. In general these tend to be of rather poor quality or downright 'tatty' and tired-looking. Make sure anything you select is good enough to enhance the school environment and stimulate learning.

Asking among the staff can often result in a really interesting selection of artefacts, pots, carved figures, fabrics etc. that can be added to the collection.

Most schools, if the truth is known, seem to have a motley collection of vases or flower containers. Sometimes these can be of value in a wider sense. Look at them and classify them carefully. There may be examples of glass (pressed or moulded, perhaps cut glass, coloured or decorated), pottery (handcrafted, moulded, jug or bowl-shaped etc.) or plastic, stone, slate, wood or basketry etc. Some may be of historical significance because of their style. Try to establish a collection which has a rich variety of types and materials and you will have resources that can be used in a wider sense than just for flowers.

It is also useful to build up a selection of fabrics which can be used to cover tables or horizontal surfaces or to act as drapery to complement any display. Sometimes these fabrics can form the focus of the display in their own right. For instance, if children were looking at the printing process and experimenting with their own print-making (see Chapter Three, 'Printmaking'), an area

136 Chapter 10

devoted to prints should include fabrics which have been printed. Similarly if work on batik (see Chapter Five, 'Textiles') is undertaken, children would benefit from examining examples of fabric decorated in this way, or printed in the same style. This gives an opportunity to study patterns and designs from other lands and provides an excellent chance to give a high profile to the artistic achievements of other cultures, developing a multicultural dimension in a natural way.

It is also important to develop a collection of natural objects, for example, seedheads, shells, interesting stones, skulls and bones, driftwood from the beach, pinecones, cork etc. These can all be used as stimuli for drawing and a range of other work, and also will greatly enhance displays and the environment of the school.

Storing resources

All the resources referred to above will need storage facilities. Careful thought needs to be given to this provision so that artefacts are readily accessible but safely housed. Fabrics are best stored folded neatly and arranged either on shelves or across coat-hangers on a rail of some sort. Some sort of easy classification helps, perhaps by colour. All items should have a sticky label attached, giving some indication of their origin and special features (for example, 'West African carving in ebony' or 'Nigerian batik fabric made with a mud resist and indigo dyes, 1990'). Schools would be wise to adopt 'house rules' which require borrowers to wash and iron fabrics after use as material attracts dust like magnets in busy classrooms and corridor areas.

Other artefacts need definite homes too. It may be possible that certain items have fairly permanent positions, such as large ceramic items standing in an entrance hall or a selection of different vases along a corridor. Other items will need storage. A cupboard or suitable shelving is probably the best idea. If this is sited in a suitable place, the shelves can be labelled and even set out like a museum resource bank, making selection and return simple.

Developing the school environment 137

ACTIVITIES

1. The art trail

Objective
To extend understanding of a range of media.

Age range
Seven to eleven.

Group size
Whole class working in smaller groups.

Time
Two hours initially and then subsequent sessions.

What you need
A selection of completed work (this can be from one class, year or from the whole school), a selection of prints and posters or photographs, paper for mounting, adhesive, clip frames or similar, paper, pens, art reference books, chalkboard, word processor (optional), Post-It notes.

What to do
Arrange the work around the classroom on desks or on a clear floor area. Explain to the children that many places have nature trails and history trails. Some places are now beginning to develop art trails. For example, some of the big cruise ships and hotels have established these as attractions. Tell the children that you are going to create your own art trail in school so that other classes can walk around the 'course' and learn about different types of art and artists.

Discuss the kinds of exhibit that would be interesting. Draw out the idea that there should be a wide range of art including three-dimensional examples – weaving, sculpture and ceramics etc. List these on the board or on paper. Add the different types of painting and drawing that could be included, remembering to consider the use of different paints and drawing tools, the use of prints, patterns, collage,

work in inks and mixed media etc. List as many varied examples as you can, even if you think it will be difficult to obtain an example to use in school.

Now ask the children to look at the specimen collection displayed around the classroom. If space is tight, ask the groups to look only at the work nearest them. When the children have studied the collection, ask them to match the list on the board with the examples they have, writing down the titles of any good specimens for later reference. When they have examined all the available artworks, hold up the prints, posters and photographs one at a time and ask the children to classify them. Try to give the children the correct title of the work and sufficient information to help them make a judgement, for example, 'This is a print of a watercolour painting by John Piper. He has also used gouache and inks. It is a painting of a famous church tower in Somerset and he painted it in about 1958.' (It is important to introduce descriptions at this stage as the children need to have an idea of how to describe other work as the art trail develops.) With the children's help, list examples alongside the categories on the board or write down new ones as they appear. Work through a range of children's work, posters, prints and photographs (which might be of children's past work) to provide a good mixed range.

Ask the groups to decide how many exhibits they would like to include in the art trail, whereabouts in the school they could be displayed and how best to do this. Get them to consider carefully what sort of exhibit should be included. Give them a few minutes to discuss this and to write down their ideas and then ask them to report back to the whole class. (The links with speaking and listening skills are obvious here and should be well exploited.) Listen to all the ideas and make a note of any things which will need later investigation, such as a survey of how much corridor

Developing the school environment **139**

wall space exists or where displays could be arranged for three-dimensional exhibits. The children can be allowed to follow up these essential queries later.

Explain that the children can make a start on choosing some items now and gradually increase the collection and develop the art trail over a period of time, filling in any obvious gaps with good examples as they are found. Ask each group to nominate two or three items they would wish to include from the available exhibits. Some groups will probably choose the same examples. Don't worry about this, it is good that there is agreement. When all the choices have been made, give each group the exhibits of their choice, or negotiate so that each group has at least one example. Now ask them to discuss together and write down appropriate accompanying information which will be mounted beside the exhibit on the art trail. Refer back to the descriptions you gave with each one you held up.

Explain that they may need to look up extra information and add anything that would be especially interesting. Provide an example to help them, such as 'John Piper trained for the legal profession like his father, but gave this up to be an artist. He loved architecture and buildings. You can see this in his paintings. He also loved the opera and ballet and often designed sets for the stage. His work is often dark but always rich in colour. He died in 1992.'

Where the exhibit is by one of the children, the group will need to ask the artist themselves for information about the work. For example, the artists could give their ideas on why they chose to produce their work in a particular way, what they were trying to show and why they chose particular colours. Explain that the information need not be complicated and that just a few lines will do. Check the descriptions and get the children to re-draft them if necessary, then let them write them out neatly or print them on a word processor. Help the groups to mount the descriptions on card, ready to accompany the exhibit.

Examples of children's work will need careful mounting and

140 Chapter 10

presenting. Prints and posters will need similar care if they are to last well. (Large clip frames from DIY shops are probably the quickest and cheapest way of doing this.) As each exhibit is ready for display, ask the group concerned to choose a suitable place to display it and ask them to mark the place with a Post-It note. (This leaves you free to choose a quiet time to complete the hanging at a later hour.)

Try to add to the collection over a period of time, looking at the original lists to see which categories are missing. Ask the children to look out for examples, or better still try to create them personally. For example, if there is no example of printing on fabric, the children could be asked to collect printed materials, research into the work of William Morris and copy out some of his designs or experiment with printmaking themselves (see Chapter Three). Alternatively they might look to see if any other classes in the school have some good examples.

Further activities
• Make a temporary exhibition on a particular subject, such as 'Animals', or 'Buildings', or have a seasonal theme.
• Dedicate the art trail to a particular period (eg. Victorian painters) and link it to a historical topic.
• Choose a specific art form for the trail, for example, all watercolour paintings or fabric designs.
• Ask each child to contribute, either generally or on a set theme.
• If the building layout permits, organise the exhibition so that examples are displayed *against* the windows looking outwards so that you can walk round the outside of the building to see the trail.
• Where the trail contains a wide range of artists selected from an extensive period of time, display the works in chronological order. Intersperse the exhibits with information about major events at that period to give the historical flavour and to create an art timeline.
• Devote the trail to work inspired by a particular culture. For example, a trail based on African art and design could include Picasso's work based on this source and the children's own responses to the same stimulus.
• Have a totally three-dimensional trail and encourage the children to overcome the problems posed in displaying this sort of exhibit by using technological skills.

Developing the school environment **141**

2. The great outdoor sculpture trail

Objective
To enhance the school grounds and widen the children's experience of sculpted forms.

Age range
Five to eleven.

Group size
Whole class working in groups.

Time
Up to two hours.

What you need
Prints and photographs of sculpture in the environment e.g. the work of Andy Goldsworthy and Grizedale Forest sculpture park artists), collections of natural items (such as stones, gravel, twigs, branches and bark, preferably found in the school grounds), fine string or wire, a camera, drawing pencils, paper, card, scissors, lolly sticks, small polythene bags or clear adhesive plastic film.

What to do
Show the children illustrations of the work of sculptors who use natural materials to make sculpted forms in the environment. Talk about artists who use a range of natural materials (often found at the site, but not necessarily), to create interesting patterns, shapes and representations which are designed to enhance the environment. Explain that this work is not necessarily permanent; for example, some artists, like Andy Goldsworthy, even work in ice and other materials which will change or rot away over time. Discuss how a record could be made of such work and how different sculptures might change over time, how they might be affected by weathering, or how they might look different as the seasons change.

Take the class out into the school grounds and ask them to work in groups to look for any natural materials they might be able to use for their artwork. Explain that they must not break anything off a living plant. Ask them to select one particular sort of material, or to select only one or two varieties and use these to create an interesting pattern on the ground. Stop them at regular intervals and gather the children around each pattern in turn and ask the artists to talk about their ideas. Encourage the rest of the children to ask questions such as:
• Why did you choose pine-cones and pebbles?
• How big are you going to make it?
• How have you stopped the leaves blowing away?

Circulate around the groups as they work and take photographs of their work in progress. Once a basic pattern begins to emerge, ask the children to start to build a natural sculpture, fastening the parts together with wire or string to create the three-dimensional structure.

Remember to stop regularly for on-site discussions and especially encourage children to explain how they have overcome the problems of joining materials and keeping them in place. Repeat the photographic records as work progresses. When the children feel they have completed their sculpture, ask them to make drawings of their work.

Leave the sculptures in place and get the children to make a small notice giving their sculpture's title and the names of the artists. Let all the other children in school know that these sculptures are in place and ask them not to touch them (unless the artists have chosen to create a 'feely work'). Make some 'Eyes on, hands off' signs to encourage visual appreciation.

Ask the children to mount their sketches of the sculptures and arrange them on a display board together with the photographs. Make sure they title their work and ask them to add a brief description, including the materials used, the size and any special features. Give them an example, such as 'Swirly tornado – patterns of swirling shapes like a big storm in the sky. We chose gravel and different sized stones arranged to show the shapes and built them up in heaps to make the patterns more interesting and powerful. It measures 2 metres by 1 metre by 20 centimetres at its highest point.'

Ask the class to read and check each description and to decide if there is sufficient information. Once they are satisfied with the descriptions, give each group a number and ask them to copy this with their detailed information on to card and cover it in polythene or adhesive clear plastic film to make it waterproof. Help them to fasten the card securely to the lolly sticks. Make a record of each number on the display board next to their sketches, then let the groups put their signs firmly in the ground beside their work.

Finally, get the class to prepare a diagram of the school grounds and the positions of all the sculptures, complete with numbers. This should be displayed next to the sketches and photographs to act as both a record of and a guide to the trail. The sculptures can either be left in place so that the effect of weathering and other effects can be noticed, or developed or replaced as decided by the children themselves.

Further activities
- Use IT to produce leaflets for other children and visitors to the trail.
- Set up a large display of the photographs and sketches of the sculptures plus photographs of the way the sculptures change over time, due to weathering etc.
- Repeat the process on a whole-school basis with different classes taking responsibility for different areas.
- Make sculptural forms with 'foreign' items like sea shells, offcuts of wood or plastic, polythene sheeting (make sure this is fixed firmly or you may have problems with neighbours!), plastic piping, slates, feathers, bones etc.

Developing the school environment

3. Art gardens

Objective
To enhance the environment and encourage children to look at colour.

Age range
Five to eleven.

Group size
Whole class working in groups.

Time
One hour initially and then subsequent sessions.

What you need
A collection of prints by different artists (at least two examples of each artist, such as Monet, Van Gogh, Turner, Picasso, Piper, Gauguin and Dufy), a small area of the school garden, garden supplies catalogues, scissors, adhesive paper, pencils, paints, collage materials, writing materials, envelopes, chalkboard, seed boxes, gardening equipment, camera (optional).

What to do
This activity should be undertaken in the spring term as you need to commence work in the growing season. The initial activities will take about an hour, but remember that it is an ongoing project.

Explain to the children that they are going to design a class garden based on the favourite colours of a particular artist. Show the children a selection of prints and organise a vote on which artist they will choose. Make sure you draw their attention to the sorts of colours each artist uses.

Ask one group of children to draw a plan of the garden patch and to paint in patterns using the colours they think their artist would choose for the flowers and plants in the garden. Ask the rest of the class to draw the garden plan and cut out from the garden catalogues pictures of plants and flowers in the colours they think their artist would choose. From time to time, stop the class and ask the children to compare and discuss their choices.

Ask the children to look at possible choices of plants and make lists of their names and colours on the board. Add the time of year the plants will be in flower. For example:
• Pansies – blue, purple, maroon, yellow, cream. Bloom in winter and spring.
• Cornflowers – bright blue. Bloom in summer.

When the lists are complete, ask the children to decide which plants bloom at the same time and group them together. Next ask them to sort the plants according to which ones are easy to grow, which can be grown from seed and which are rather expensive. Keep all the initial colour pictures and lists as a guide.

Ask the children if they can think of anyone who could help you by giving you plants or seeds for your garden, then let them write letters to parents, friends, the headteacher, governors, the PTA or anyone else they can think of in the community to explain the project and ask for help!

Discuss the things which should be included in these letters and write up a list of useful words on the board.

Older children can be asked to draft out letters and work on them until they are ready to take home or send to appropriate recipients. With younger children this work could be linked with a handwriting exercise or you could act as scribe. The links with English are obviously very strong.

Don't worry if the cost of the project seems likely to be high. Most colours can actually be created fairly cheaply from seeds. Seeds of sunflowers (perfect for Van Gogh), nasturtiums, candytuft, lobelia, love-lies-bleeding and sweet peas are cheap and easily available. Parents and friends are often generous with surplus bedding plants.

Make and display a large diagram of the plot. Discuss this with the children and ask them to decide where the different blocks of colour are to go in the garden area. Explain that the garden cannot be created quickly and that they will need to obtain the plants gradually and work on the project bit by bit. Add the children's plans and initial pictures to the display.

Over the course of the next few weeks, collect seeds and let the children plant them according to the directions on the packet, either in seed boxes or directly into the prepared ground. Give different groups in the class responsibility for the nurture of particular boxes or patches. As the garden progresses, let the children record developments on the display. When the seeds have grown sufficiently, help the children plant the flowers out, according to the cultivation instructions, to match the diagram. Get the groups to take turns to tend the garden. If possible, take regular photographs of the developments and changes in growth.

Use the garden and individual flowers as the subject for children's painting, drawing and collage. Compare these pictures with the initial designs and ask the children to comment on the similarities and differences.

Further activities
- Develop a whole-school project, with each class cultivating a separate garden area, using the same theme or just choosing one colour.
- Include a painting in waterproof paints on a wooden or weatherproof background to act as the focal point of the garden. This could be in the style of a particular painter, a copy of part or all of a particular painting, or just on a colour theme.
- If a whole-garden project is too complex, let the children grow plants in window boxes or flower-pots, basing their colour schemes on the same idea.
- Make indoor gardens using flowers made out of paper or fabric, using the same idea to develop colour schemes. Display them on the window sills.

Developing the school environment   **145**

4. Murals

Objective
To enhance the school environment and investigate the techniques of wall-painting and working with large surfaces.

Age range
Five to eleven.

Group size
Whole class working in groups.

Time
One hour plus subsequent sessions.

What you need
A large expanse of wall or a very large section of plain coloured fabric which can be stretched and mounted on to a wall area, illustrations of large murals or wall-paintings include *trompe-l'oeil* examples (the work of Spencer, Whistler, eighteenth century interior designers and twentieth century inner city wall artists would be useful), drawing paper, pencils, A2 sheets of paper, newspaper, overhead projector (optional), paints, water pots, mixing trays. For a mural: chalk, a selection of brushes from ½" to 4" width, weatherproof paints (not gloss), a selection of emulsion paints, foil takeaway trays, PVA medium. For a fabric hanging: a large eyeletting kit, plastic-coated cuphooks (two for each 20cm width of fabric), two strips of wood batten 1½" x ½" width of fabric, tools to fix the hanging to the wall, sewing equipment.

What to do
Choose a wall area, either interior or exterior, where an interesting mural would be a focal point. Often there are rather drab areas around school buildings which would benefit from a bright and intriguing design. The chosen area could be a wall that is full of windows, doorways or other wall 'furniture', or it could be a particularly dull part of a corridor, cloakroom or changing area. Seek the approval of the headteacher to undertake the mural project before you commence wielding the first paintbrush.

Decide whether you will get the children to paint directly on to the wall itself (generally necessary if the wall is cluttered with windows etc.) or whether it would be better to make a removable 'mural'

painted on fabric which can be stretched between fixed battens.

Tell the children that they are going to undertake a large scale painting to enhance the school environment. Explain that ever since the earliest cave paintings there have been decorations added to large wall surfaces. Talk about the wall-paintings of the Greeks, the Romans and the Egyptians, the beautiful murals in medieval churches, the magnificent and elaborate painted interiors of mosques etc. Ask the children if they have seen other examples. They may have seen murals in shopping centres or on large buildings. Discuss why people sometimes choose to decorate large expanses of ugly wall. Show the children some examples of murals and if possible, some *trompe-l'oeil*.

Show the children the area of wall where they will make their mural. Discuss possible ideas. Ask them to think about some important questions and prompt them if necessary.
• Is the area ugly, or dull, or dark?
• What sort of picture, pattern or *trompe-l'oeil* decorations would make it more interesting and attractive.
• Is there any logical theme that might be used, such as school activities or the local area? Is the school close to a historical or geographically important site? Is there a particular sort of wildlife in the area? Is there a famous local industry? Or regional crafts, foods, products etc?

Encourage lots of discussion and ideas at this stage to stimulate really imaginative responses.

Let the children work in groups to discuss their ideas and draw some possible designs, making notes of why they have decided on a particular design, so that they can later report back to the rest of the class. Give each group a large sheet of paper and ask them to draw out their chosen mural design, painting it in the colours they feel will be most appropriate. These should be completed and left to dry.

Explain to the children that artists would make many different planning drawings and then possibly several paint 'studies' before they decided on their final choice. Explain also that sometimes designs were commissioned and that the commissioning person would look at a selection of possible pictures from which the actual work would be chosen. Now tell the class that they are going to choose a final design. Ask each group to hold up their paintings in turn and to share their ideas with the rest of the class. Ask the class only to give positive comments. Help

Developing the school environment **147**

them by asking them what they like about each exhibit. Let the children consider all the designs and then ask them what they like about each exhibit. Let the children consider all the designs and then ask them how they can choose one. They may, for example, decide to organise a vote or even to canvass opinion. If they wish to consult others in the school, make a display of all the designs together with the artists' notes and ask the children to conduct a survey.

Once a final decision has been made, explain to the children that the design can now be transferred to the wall or the fabric. Young children will not be able to transfer the design directly to the wall or fabric themselves, and it might be easier for older children to be involved in the painting of a wall surface. Older children in school, children from the local secondary school, students from the nearest college or adult helpers can be involved with this stage. However, even quite young children can paint directly on to fabric if it has previously been marked out with a line design and than laid over newspapers on a floor and painted small sections at a time.

If the children are to make a mural, draw a grid on the wall area using chalk. Then, working one square at a time, use the original design as a guide and enlarge the picture directly on to the wall, chalking heavily to ensure a strong outline. Alternatively, if the mural is to be painted on an interior wall, trace the design on to an overhead projector transparency, project it on to the wall and carefully chalk around the outline. The design can be transferred to fabric using either of these methods, but the easiest way is to lie the material on the hall floor and use the squaring up method.

When the rough design is ready, let the children begin the painting. Tip small, easily manageable amounts of emulsion paint into old foil containers. These are easier to work with and cause less damage if they are tipped. Remember that these paints can be mixed together to make new shades. (If a large amount of one colour is needed, make sure this is mixed at the same time to ensure colour consistency. The bulk of it can be poured into separate containers and kept for later use.) Ask the children to work only on small sections at a time. If you have more than one person painting at the same time, make sure they have sufficient space to work in and do not get in each other's way. Do not rush this exercise and ask the children to check on how work is progressing at regular

148 Chapter 10

intervals, for instance, at each playtime. Children may need adult help with painting high sections of the mural but do try to involve them in the painting of safer, lower sections if possible. However, even if this is not feasible, the children themselves will still have been the designers and will enjoy seeing their own ideas come to life.

If you are using fabric, let only a few children work at the same time and keep them well away from each other's area. Try to arrange to have the fabric left undisturbed in one place until it is completely finished. The fabric can also be painted with emulsion paint. This will dry fairly quickly but avoid moving it until the material has had an overnight drying period.

When the mural is completed and has dried thoroughly, paint over it with a medium consistency solution of PVA adhesive to seal it and provide a lightly varnished finish.

The fabric mural will need neatening at the edges. This can be done either by sewing a neat seam around all the edges or by sticking down a 'hem' using undiluted PVA. Next fix the battens to the wall at the top first of all. The cuphooks should be screwed in at about 20cm intervals. Large eyelets should be inserted in the fabric at the same intervals to match. Hang the mural from these and stretch it tightly, marking the place for the bottom battening to be fixed. Fasten the wood to the correct place and fasten the cuphooks, again at 20cm intervals, along the underside of the batten (Figure 1) for safety's sake. Complete the matching eyelets on the bottom edge of the mural and stretch it down and over the hooks.

Further activities

• Choose a theme and create several murals in different styles (eg birds and animals painted in the style of different painters such as Rousseau, Chagall, Marc, Stubbs etc.).
• Restrict each mural to certain colour themes.
• Create four murals representing the seasons.
• Create four murals representing the elements fire, earth, air and water.
• Add appliqué sections to fabric murals to produce a three-dimensional effect.

Figure 1

Developing the school environment 149

5. Three-dimensional murals

Objective
To enhance the school environment and look at three-dimensional wall embellishment.

Age range
Five to eleven.

Group size
Whole class working in pairs or small groups.

Time
One to three hours.

What you need
A collection of wooden offcuts of varying shapes and sizes, measuring tape, a selection of emulsion paints, pictures of examples of abstract art, brushes, paint containers, mixing pots, good quality exterior varnish, chalk, tools for wall-fixing, polythene work surface covering, plastic binliners, adhesive labels.

What to do
Explain to the children that you are going to build up a three-dimensional mural to brighten up the school environment. As with the previous activity, it is useful to spend some time walking around the school exterior and interior areas with the children looking for places which would benefit from the addition of a suitable mural. The chosen area can be large or small and the offcuts available can often lend themselves to particular areas. However, do not let yourself be totally restricted by this. Quite small offcuts can be very effectively grouped in profusion to make really dynamic displays on quite large expanses of wall. When you have decided on which area is to be used, make a note of the measurements.

Ask the children to look at the work of artists who have used abstract ideas in their work, using shapes and colour blocks in exciting ways. Let the children look at the work of a range of artists if possible. This might include Paul Klee, Picasso, Matisse, Braque, Mondrian and Kasimir Malevich. Do not worry if you find the work hard to understand – children are much more flexible in their thinking than adults. Explain that many artists have tried to reduce their representations into the simplest possible shapes or that they merely enjoy experimenting with shape and colour and the position of one part of their work with another.

Next give the children the offcuts to look at. Ask them to sort through the various shapes until they find one they particularly like. Ask them to describe the shape to a partner and to say what they like about it. Help them with questions, such as:
• Does it look like anything in particular?
• Is it curved or straight or a mixture?

- Is it all the same width throughout?
- Does the shape suggest a mood, eg. happy, angry?

Ask the children to find another piece that could be placed alongside the first one, or be attached to it, and would develop the shape. Ask them to work in pairs or small groups to arrange their offcuts on their desks in an interesting way. Spend a few minutes looking at all the group patterns, remembering to let the 'artists' themselves explain why they have chosen the layout.

Now explain that these offcuts can be painted in plain colours or patterns, or simply varnished to bring out the colour of the wood. Ask the children to consider how they could make their arrangements more exciting by working in this way. (If the children want to experiment before painting their pieces, let them draw round their shapes on paper and have a practice run first.) Let each group paint their sections and leave them to dry on a covered worksurface.

Remember that emulsion paints can be mixed and, as they dry fairly quickly, overlay colours and patterns can be added within an hour or two.

If the mural is to be placed outside or in any area where it is likely to get worn down, or if it will be difficult to keep clean, varnish the dry pieces. Leave these to dry thoroughly on a polythene sheet (to prevent them sticking) overnight.

Once the pieces are dry, the final assembly can take place. Use chalk to mark out an area in the hall, or on the playground, the same dimensions as the wall to be used. Divide this up into squares. Get the children to prepare a large paper plan marked out in the same way. Explain that this will form the working diagram when it is time for fixing. Let each group of children arrange their part of the mural on the grid where they feel it will look most effective. Encourage the groups to experiment with overlapping or intertwining their work with those of others, or to place their section somewhere where it will balance others'. However, stress that the work should look like one complete mural when it is finished, rather than lots of little ones. When the final design has been laid out, ask all the children to stand around it and comment on the arrangement. Let any suggestions for redesigning the layout be discussed and make any decisions by a democratic process.

Use the large plan to record carefully where each piece is to go. Use a grid system to identify each square and link this with both maths and geography mapping skills. Write the square grid number on the back of each offcut to help later identification and then put the pieces for each

Developing the school environment **151**

square into one plastic bag.

Fixing the design to the wall will obviously be too difficult for the children but presents an ideal opportunity to involve parents, colleagues, secondary children or members of the community to help. The wall will need to be marked out in chalked squares to match the plan and each part should be worked on in turn. The children themselves can help by sorting out the pieces for each square as it is fixed and by supervising their section.

Further activities

• Look at the work of Victor Pasmore (who specialised in working with wooden pieces) and also Louise Nevelson (*Royal Tidt 5*) who created arrangements of offcuts within a box structure. Children could create their own boxes following this idea.
• Choose a single colour theme and work in shades of the same colour. In this way you can develop different colour walls around the school, which can be very attractive and a good resource for further learning for the youngest children.
• Limit the colours to only two for a really dynamic effect to encourage careful use of the juxtaposition of pieces.
• Design a representational mural using carefully chosen shapes and supplement this with wall painting in between the shapes.
• Restrict shapes to specified forms (eg. geometrical, geographical, astronomical) and have these specially cut ready for painting.
• Choose a wide selection of different woods and ask the children to varnish rather than paint them to enhance the different colours and grain. Ask the children to add labels to identify the different types of wood used.

CHAPTER 11

Curriculum planning and assessment

As with every other subject in the National Curriculum, there is a need for a whole-school policy on art and sound curriculum planning. Naturally a curriculum co-ordinator is essential to support and guide teachers, to take a lead in staff INSET arrangements, to help in the development of assessment and recording procedures and to ensure the overseeing and regular review of implementation. This can be a tall order when many teachers feel anxious about their own artistic abilities or knowledge of art! However, the good news is that teachers do not need to be highly talented artists in their own right with a mass of well-tried techniques at their fingertips. Such techniques can be learned and experimented with alongside the children. It cannot be denied that teachers can gradually acquire this wider knowledge as they plan, and indeed, they can share much excitement discovering more about art and artists with their classes, building up a bank of experience and resources as they go. This chapter is designed to help teachers, and the art co-ordinator in particular, to address the issues and find a clear way forward.

The first step should be to undertake a school audit for art. The art co-ordinator will need to be aware of the following points:
• what staff expertise exists;
• what equipment and resources exist;
• what storage arrangements are in place;
• what budget is available;
• what books, prints and paintings exist;
• what parental/governor interests and skills might be available;
• what original National Curriculum policies might be in place.

All these factors will need to be considered and should help in developing a sound policy.

Curriculum planning and assessment 153

BACKGROUND

The school art policy

All curriculum planning must relate to the Art Statutory Orders but should also relate to the school's own art policy. It is essential that this policy is drawn up and shared with all staff in a planned way because it should form a vital support mechanism for teachers in their work with children. In many schools the writing of such a policy will be the responsibility of the art co-ordinator. Sometimes they may be able to call upon a small working party to help them in this task, and where this is possible, it is obviously preferable.

The art policy should not be confused with a scheme of work. It should address issues which relate to the teaching of art within the school in a general way, considering broad aims and issues. It should set a context that is unlikely to alter even if the actual choice of content changes in school. The scheme of work would be a more particular and detailed schedule of specific content and timings. Schools may wish to develop a scheme of work but this should use the art policy as a point of reference.

The art policy should address a range of issues including the following points.

The place of art in the curriculum

The policy should recognise that art is not just a 'service' subject, designed to provide illustrations for other areas (eg. 'Now draw a picture when you've finished your work') but a fully fledged part of a child's entitlement. It should address the importance of the development of a visual literacy which is a vital element of a child's education – ever more so in a world that requires responses to, and interpretation of, an enormous range of visual stimuli – television, video, computer graphics, pictorial representations and film.

It should stress art's natural links with other areas of the curriculum but highlight strongly that children need to learn *about* art as well as *through* art. For instance, a child needs to learn how to use different tools and materials with confidence. They can do this effectively in the context of a study of Aztec culture (acting very much as archaeologists exploring artefacts) but they also need real opportunities to experiment with making their own interpretations,

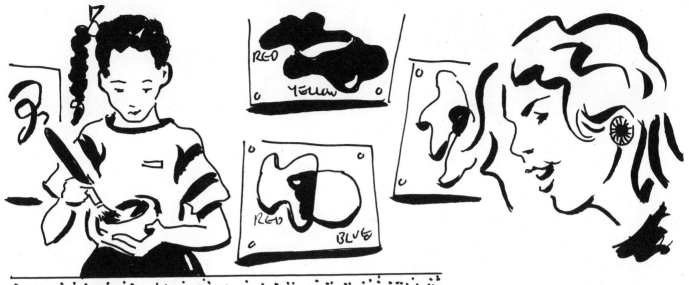

developing new skills and evaluating their own artistic outcomes.

The links between close observational skills and reading, science and technology, plus the development of fine co-ordination and manipulative skills and handwriting might also be recognised.

Continuity and progression

The necessity of building on children's previous work and of developing skills, experience and ideas further needs clear articulation, as do the implications for establishing a simple, manageable form of record-keeping which identifies the range of work undertaken. This might mean an agreed system of developing individual children's portfolios of work, the use of sketch books and photographs etc. (Reference might be made here to the establishment of a scheme of work which will match with other areas of the school's planning, but it is better not to include this in full detail.)

Assessment

This section of the policy should address the issues of teacher assessment as an ongoing process, not leaving it to teachers at the end of each Key Stage. Schools also need to have clear policies on how children can be involved in their own assessment, especially as evaluation of their own work forms such an integral part of the National Curriculum for Art.

Differentiation

Many of the activities undertaken in art will lead to differentiation by outcome (each child following the same task and achieving their own level of outcome) but teachers also need to plan particular activities to enable individual children to progress in specific areas. In other words, teachers will need to devise different activities for different pupils or 'differentiation by task'. For instance, a child who needs to develop close observational skills would need activities to promote this, whereas another child might need to concentrate on looking at tonal qualities, while yet another would be helped by working on colour mixing and matching.

Children with learning difficulties are often liberated by being able to use art as a means of recording. This presents wonderful opportunities for language development – if the teacher plans to work alongside at this time. In the same way, differentiated activities need to be planned in to ensure children of higher abilities have sufficient challenge.

Planning and organisation

The teacher's planning should reflect the specific aims of activities and ensure that all children have, over a period of time, opportunities to work in a variety of ways (individually,

Curriculum planning and assessment **155**

groups, whole class) and have adequate input and guidance from the teacher. Often very busy class teachers rely on painting, modelling or other art activities, especially in groups, to keep children happily occupied with little teacher interaction. It is essential that the teacher uses skills and well-timed intervention to bring a quality to children's understanding and practical work. Such critical intervention might be:
• to show how different techniques can be used;
• to demonstrate the safe and proper use of tools;
• to ask the children to describe their work to others;
• to discuss individual ideas and share comment;
• to draw attention to particular developments reference materials etc.;
• to help children assess and evaluate their own work.

The development of support staff and adults other than teachers will also need addressing, in particular ways in which 'helpers' can be briefed to understand the aims behind any specific activity and the points of discussion, vocabulary etc. that need highlighting when working with the pupils.

Often activities can be planned to sit comfortably with other topics or themes being studied. However, it is vital that the art element is properly developed and not just used to add colour to the project. This can be achieved with careful forethought. For instance, geographical work can be reinforced and art skills developed by asking children to compare different artists' interpretations of landscape painting, allied to their own representations of local geographical features and perhaps an investigation into the properties of local materials. A project on the Victorians could include a study of the Pre-Raphaelites and their work ideas, with children concentrating on close observational skills and working with nature. Work set in a historical context naturally needs to be placed against a timeline for reference and the development of chronological skills.

The organisation of the classroom also needs consideration. The policy should indicate the need for adequate planning for the siting of art activities, the joint use of practical areas and the necessity for classroom 'house rules' for safety, clearing up and storage. It might also indicate the time available for art activities, the school's arrangements for display and the accessibility of resources throughout the school and other organisational issues pertinent to the particular establishment.

Safety

There should be a section of the art policy which addresses the issue of safety, both in general terms and within the special context of the school. For instance, there may be particular difficulties regarding children moving about in open practical areas or there may need to be special guidelines for the use of certain equipment, such as the kiln.

Resources

This will be an important area and there will need to be much staff discussion about general requirements and storage. For instance, it may be that the use of a range of drawing pencils is a new venture in the school. Teachers should be aware that children need to experience using these tools, and they should know what is available, where the pencils are housed and how they can access them. Similarly they need to know what reference material is available and what artefacts, paintings, artworks, prints, posters, slides, fabrics and other support materials are ready for use. There might also be some commitment indicated to the future planned provision of new resources, such as the annual planned purchase of art reference books to supplement the library.

Reference could be made to the use of adults other than teachers and to local resources such as links with the general community, colleges, galleries and artists in residence within school. The policy should make clear statements about the provision of visits to exhibitions etc. and the use of particular visitors to school. Similarly it would be helpful for teachers to know what help is available within school – who to call upon for advice or for finding appropriate INSET and what planned programmes of support are scheduled for staff development.

There also might be a section on display and presentation. This might concern staff responsibilities for particular areas of the school or for taking work into the community (such as links with the local churches, libraries or other feeder schools).

Other areas

This list is not definitive. There may be other vital areas that schools may wish to add. As with all such policies, the most important activity will be staff consultation and discussion and any activities which allow the staff to take

Curriculum planning and assessment 157

ownership of its text. That is why it is important, even if the co-ordinator has written the initial document, that adequate time is found to consider the policy as a staff. It also follows, of course, that new teachers joining the school should have the opportunity to go through the policy personally with the responsible co-ordinator who can amplify any sections as needed.

Building art into the curriculum

Most schools have spent lengthy periods of time putting the core subjects and technology, history and geography in place. Fairly extensive programmes have been devised, either in a thematic approach or on a more traditional subject-based timetable. The art co-ordinator might feel that there is little space or leeway left for art! However, the programmes of study for art need to be followed adequately to enable teachers to give accurate assessments at the end of each Key Stage. So how can art be fitted in appropriately?

With time such a precious commodity, nobody wishes to 're-invent the wheel' and it may be that current school planning will easily accommodate some, if not all, areas of art. First of all the co-ordinator, preferably working with a small team, should look at each Key Stage phase programme and try to match the planned topic areas with the art programmes of study. For example, if we consider Key Stage 1, most children will be looking closely at plants and flowers and naming the different parts and also studying 'minibeasts' and other animals as part of their science work, either as part of a wider project or in discrete subject slots. This work presents a perfect opportunity for young children to:
• record observations from direct experience of the natural environment;
• select and sort items.

These are both parts of the Programme of Study for AT1, Investigating and Making. They could learn to use a range of drawing pencils and record what they have found. They could go on to use paint to represent the flowers, they could use simple printmaking techniques to print plant designs, they could translate these initial paintings and drawings into claywork or textile collage or embroidery and thread work – all activities which give opportunities for the development of skills while enhancing their knowledge and understanding of science work. This could be easily developed further to involve a comparison of the way other artists (such as the

examples given in the Statutory Orders – William Morris and Vincent Van Gogh) have illustrated flowers (in particular their different styles or ways they have used colour) and how their own pictures compare with the artists' work. In this way teachers can begin to address AT2, Knowledge and Understanding.

It is important that the two ATs are not seen as entirely separate. Wherever possible, they should intertwine. A common theme for Key Stage 1 is 'Me', or perhaps 'The Family'. There are the obvious links with History in looking at photographs of the child taken from babyhood to the present time and those of the family, probably spanning a greater period of time. There are opportunities to look at treasured artefacts from the past – perhaps beloved cuddly creatures, old books and toys that have been in the family etc. It would be relatively easy to extend this work to include the close observational skills referred to above, plus other developments, such as painting Dad as a small child or an imaginary self-portrait of the child at Dad's present age, or the design of their bedrooms at the same period (AT1). Older photographs lend themselves to stimulus for children to learn about tone by asking them to paint their own portraits in only black and white or sepia tones. This could lead on to looking at paintings or illustrations of children or families through the ages or at a particular period in time.

Geographical work might centre on the immediate locality (Geography, Places) and this too could be extended by asking children to imagine what the area looked like before the houses were built, or linking it into a local visit, and to paint, draw or represent their ideas. This could naturally lead on to children learning to mix and use a range of earth colours, and to observe the masses of different greens in nature. A further development could be looking at a range of paintings of houses through the ages, or landscapes and industrial scenes, applicable to ATs 1 and 2.

In the same way, a study of 'Weather' at Key Stage 1 or 2 (which might bring in Geography, Places) could include children recording different types of weather conditions in a variety of ways and also looking at other artists' interpretations or considering the work of environmental artists and the materials they choose to use. A study of the work of Turner, Money or Sisley would be appropriate at this stage.

At Key Stage 2, work for History, using a range of historical sources, would connect well with children studying artefacts and comparing different materials

Curriculum planning and assessment 159

and designs before making their own examples or records. For example, Britain Since 1930 would give ideal opportunities for children to look at 'Pop Art' and a wide range of modern artists' and designers' work in many media. The war artists, such as Nash, Spencer, Henry Moore and Barbara Hepworth, could provide useful source material for history studies.

Likewise in Geography, the contrasting locality in the UK gives opportunities to look at paintings and landscapes which are very different to the children's own area. The study of an economically developing country gives wide scope to look at the artistic heritage and culture of the chosen area, and the way in which locally available materials have affected the way artists and designers work.

Having analysed all the possible links, there may still be some areas of deficiency. There may be no natural place in which to develop some necessary skills. For instance, the Statutory Orders require children to be introduced to the work of artists, craftspeople and designers in order to develop an appreciation of our rich diverse cultural heritage with a selection of genres and styles. These should be from the locality, the past and present and from a variety of western and non-western cultures. Merely linking in with current projects, although extremely valuable, may not cover sufficiently broad a range of historical periods and cultures.

The co-ordinator will need to ensure that a suitably wide range of study of artists, craftspeople and designers work will be built into the programmes at a suitable juncture, either as a mini-project in their own right or as a discreet subject. Similarly a cohesive programme of skills, including the use of a wide range of tools and materials, need identifying and building in across the Key Stages. It is vital for teachers to realise that the skills, knowledge and opportunities for understanding art must be deliberately planned in and not left to chance. The co-ordinator has an important role to play in overseeing the school's curriculum planning and identifying the obvious links but, perhaps more importantly, those areas which must be built in especially.

Developing guidelines

Once the policy has been compiled and the co-ordinator has looked at the school's programmes for topic themes and identified appropriate links with art, these need to be shared with staff. The rolling programme of topic/theme titles can be clearly set out with the suggested art links listed alongside. These should include, where possible, names of a range of artists who could be studied and/or particular skills that could be linked to the topic (eg. close observational skills and the natural history work of Tunnicliffe, Edith Holden, Redouté).

Obviously if links have been established with other curriculum areas there are resource implications to be considered. For example, if it has been established that an investigation into the Victorians should include a study of Pre-Raphaelite paintings and artists then it will be necessary to ensure that there are sufficient resources either in school, or accessible by forward planning, to meet the needs of classes working on this area. This might include developing a bank of suitable prints which could be chosen carefully to illustrate aspects of Victorian life such as William Bell Scott's *Iron and Coal,* William Maw Egley's *Omnibus Life in London* or Ford Madox Brown's *Work* or *The Last of England.* However, reference would also need to be made to the other characteristic strands of Pre-Raphaelite work which included the representation of literary and historical events and so examples of this aspect should also be identified.

Many Pre-Raphaelite painters, notably William Holman Hunt, used religious themes for their work and this could offer a further link to RE. Naturally, adequate time should also be devoted to the style and technique of Pre-Raphaelite painters!

Of course, prints may not always be available and so other resources will need to be found. Art books will provide a rich source of information but these can be expensive. The co-ordinator will need to prioritise a list of reference materials which can be expanded and added to each year as the financial planning

Curriculum planning and assessment

takes place. But books may be available on loan from the local library service which can supplement resources – but remember to reserve these well in advance as every other school is working to the National Curriculum and may have the same idea! A newer feature of some library services is video hire and there are some exciting art videos available which give an excellent analysis of different artists' work and of different historical periods or cultures. Explore the possible use of CD Rom/CDI facilities. Consult with the librarians as they have access to catalogues that list these possibilities and generally they will obtain them for you (even purchasing them especially, if you are lucky). Do not forget too, working with a local gallery. They may have examples of a particular kind of painting or of subject matter that would be invaluable. There may be a chance to organise a visit or to arrange for a visitor to come to school.

Also there may be material resources to consider. For example, if a class were going to study the Indus Valley as part of their geographical work it would make sense to build up a collection of artefacts (costumes, decorative objects, domestic items) or illustrations of these which would give an insight into the aesthetic culture of the Indus Valley and can form valuable starting points for art.

It may also be possible gradually to build up a collection of postcards, slides and posters which will enrich both art and other areas of the curriculum. This will take time and therefore should be a planned and ongoing activity. Don't forget to take advantage of staff lucky enough to go to exciting places for their holidays! Ask them to bring back suitable photographs, pictures or fabrics etc. to add to the school resource bank – and establish a way to reimburse them for any outlay. Also remember to collect colour supplements and magazines and natural objects such as shells, seedheads etc.

There will need to be planned expenditure to ensure that there is a good range of paints, brushes, papers etc. in school and that clay is available and has adequate storage to keep it in good condition. Items such as rollers and printing inks, ceramic tools, craft knives, batik equipment, weaving materials and other specialist resources will also need to be collected, if necessary over a period of time.

It will then be necessary for a set of fairly detailed guidelines to be established to help the non-specialist teacher know how art can be planned into their work, to realise what is available to support them – both in material resources and in professional advice and the 'house rules' of using them effectively – and to know how to develop certain ideas and processes. Even if there have been extensive discussions on these aspects already, guidelines are essential as an aide-memoire to established staff and as a vital reference point for newly appointed or supply teachers.

These guidelines should not form a long prescriptive list of art activities to be followed but should be a useful reference document to aid teacher planning and organisation. It should, however, show clearly how skills can be developed and give some indication of how continuity and progression should be built into programmes throughout the school. A good format would be to take different areas of art and provide a list of planning ideas and development activities. For example, if the area being covered were drawing and mark-making, the list could include the following points.

• All children need to have opportunities at all ages to develop their close observational skills through recording through drawing. Work of this kind should be planned into every class programme.
• It should include work on line, tone, shape, pattern and texture – the formal elements of art. (Here include examples of suitable activities, preferably with photocopied illustrations from different age groups in the school. This will help teachers understand the terms and see how different classes respond at different stages of development.) Make sure the contexts of the activities illustrated are also explained eg. 'Exploring the use of graphite sticks, Year 3, National Curriculum Art'; 'Drawings of growing plants, Year 1, National Curriculum Science, Life Processes and Living Things, emphasising line'; 'Victorian artefacts drawn emphasising tone and texture, Year 5, National Curriculum History.
• Children need to experience drawing with a range of different mark-making tools. They should use and learn the different properties of drawing pencils B–8B; wax crayons; coloured pencils; aquarelle pencils (these can be dipped into water); graphite sticks, felt-tipped pens; coloured inks; pastels; a range of pens; sponges; home-made

Curriculum planning and assessment 163

mark-making tools and drawing with erasers on a scribbled pencil background. They also need to see the work of other artists working in this way and to compare and talk about their own work in drawing.
- The following mark-making materials and examples of work are available in school and arrangements for the storage and access to these materials are (here add a list of resources, available prints, books, etc, any possible wider curriculum links and special 'house rules' particular to the school. You might want to point out, for example, that children should be told to take care not to put graphite sticks in their mouths and that they need to wash their hands carefully after use).

- As children acquire increased skills in the selection and use of these tools they should be encouraged to develop their own ideas, choosing materials which will enable them to achieve particular effects and mixing media where this is appropriate. (Add examples of work across different ages showing progression or, if you are at an early stage of development and no such work exists, give examples of what this could be and/or list helpful art reference books in school.)

In this way the different areas of art can be covered and you may find the chapter headings in this book a useful basis from which to start. Non-specialist teachers might appreciate the inclusion of a Glossary section to explain artistic terminology – such as the one in this publication. It is also a good idea to make a list of what progressions of skills may have been covered to help with teacher assessment in due course. Many schools are compiling anthologies of children's work to help teachers moderate the different levels of achievement in the various subject areas of the National Curriculum. It would also be useful for the co-ordinator to compile an art anthology, selecting work from all abilities across the whole school age range to illustrate continuity and progression. This would be a very positive and useful reference point for all teachers making assessments on children's progress.

Assessment

There are no current plans to produce national tests at Key Stages 1 to 3. There are no levels of attainment to be used for assessment. In art,

164 Chapter 11

assessment is to be based on the End of Key Stage Descriptions (EKSDs). Judgements will, therefore, have to be made on the basis of the accumulated records and evidence of all teachers in each Key Stage. It will not be possible for the teachers in Year 2 and Year 6 alone to glean all the necessary evidence in their current classes on which to make such judgements. It is, therefore, important that each school develops a simple method of assessment and recording progress and experience on which other colleagues can call to plan further work. It is important that the school has a policy to decide what evidence should be amassed to help make these judgements. One of the easiest ways would be to have a portfolio of each pupil's work which might include:
• actual paintings and drawings;
• preparatory designs, sketch books;
• photographs of work and projects too bulky to keep;
• a record of practical work undertaken in different media using different techniques and how these were developed;
• evidence of the range of artist's work that has been studied with resulting practical work plus – most importantly – records of the children's own evaluation of their work.
The best method of gathering a useful bank of work to be used for assessment would be to have each piece of work accompanied by a pupils' assessment sheet. Examples of different sheets for different age groups and different types of work are given on photocopiable pages 172 to 182. The assessment of the two attainment targets should be possible from the evidence included. By having children actively involved in their assessment, teachers give them invaluable opportunities to meet the statutory requirements of ATs 1 and 2 at both Key Stages.

Curriculum planning and assessment 165

Key Stage 1, AT1 Investigating and making
• Review what they have done and describe what they might change or develop in future work.

Key Stage 1, AT2 Knowledge and understanding
• Describe works or art, craft and design in simple terms, and explain what they think and feel first.

Key Stage 2, AT1 Investigating and making
• Experiment with ideas suggested by visual and other source materials.
• Reflect on and adapt their work in the light of what they intended and consider what they might develop in further work.

Key Stage 2, AT2 Knowledge and understanding
• Compare the ideas, methods and approaches used in different styles and traditions.
• Express ideas and opinions, developing an art, craft and design vocabulary, and the ability to use knowledge to support views.

The co-ordinator's role
When a portfolio of work has been accumulated, with appropriate pupil/teacher assessment notes, it should be easy to check the evidence against the programmes of study requirements.

The co-ordinator has a consultancy role here. It would be a good idea for the co-ordinator to prepare a portfolio that could be shared with colleagues at a staff meeting to show examples of how such an anthology would simplify assessment.

The portfolio itself will be a really helpful tool for teachers to plan further work – whether it is planning activities to reinforce and develop skills (eg. the revisiting and further development of close observational skills) or to use it as a check to see that a wide variety of different media and tools have been experienced or to ensure that a range of artists, craftspeople and designers from different times and cultures has been covered with accompanying practical work. It also has an important role to play in allowing children themselves to review past examples of their own achievement and using this as a resource for checking personal progress and building on past work. They may even wish to take the example of earlier work and use it as a starting point for new, more developed ideas.

Although the portfolio itself should serve as a very useful record, a simple record sheet outlining work and experiences undertaken could supplement this, indicating a fuller range of evidence than can be selected for each portfolio. A suggested format for this appears on photocopiable pages 183 to 187.

PHOTOCOPIABLES

The pages in this section can be photocopied and adapted to suit your own needs and those of your class. They do not need to be declared in any return in respect of any photocopying licence.

Where any of the photocopiable pages relate to a specific area of the book, cross-references have been given at the top of the page.

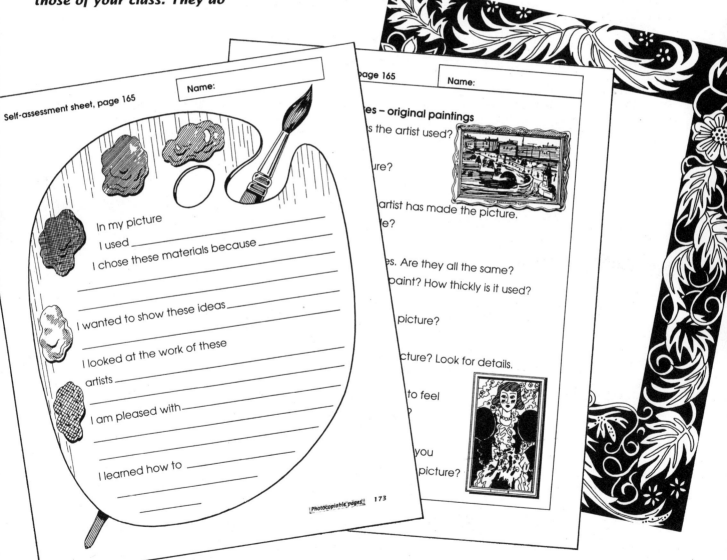

Photocopiable pages **167**

A checklist for centrally stored resources, page 10

The following items should be **available within school.** They should be stored in a readily accessible place with a system for collection and return clearly established. Any safety aspects must be recognised.

Printmaking
- A selection of water-based printing inks
- Easy Print polystyrene printing sheets
- Paint rollers

Textiles
- A range of threads and wools, preferably categorised by colour (raffia wastebins are useful)
- A range of textile samples, including multicultural examples, in reasonable lengths suitable for study and display
- Plain cloth for printing – unbleached calico, cotton etc.
- Trimmings – feathers, beads, buttons etc.
- Needles – a range of sizes and uses
- Batik pot, wax pellets and tjanting tools (small, medium and large)
- Fabric inks, paints and crayons

3D materials
- Modroc or plaster-impregnated bandage
- Plastic bowls and buckets
- Collection of old boxes, containers, cylinders etc. for modelling

Ceramics
- Rolling pins, modelling tools, tile cutters, plastic sheeting
- Selection of clay, glazes and slips
- A drying shelf – safe area for work to dry out before firing

Computer
- Access to computer with printer (preferably colour type)
- A range of software with user instructions

Reference resources
- A range of art books (containing examples of art and artists work over a broad period of history and a selection of very different artists)
- Slides, posters, prints, postcards
- Examples of real work – paintings, drawings, ceramics, design

A checklist for classroom resources, page 10

The following items should be **available to children in the classroom.** Teachers can manage 'stock control' best by ensuring that materials are organised in an easily accessible manner and that class storage systems contain only sufficient items for regular use – which are topped up as necessary. Children should be involved in the monitoring and organisation of stock, thus increasing learning opportunities.

Papers
- Good quality drawing paper (eg. cartridge) – A2, A3, A4, A5, in at least two different weights and 'tooth' (surface texture)
- Tracing paper
- A range of sugar papers – A2, A3, in different colours and shades, and with different weights
- A range of other papers – wallpaper, wrapping paper, tissue, etc. of different weights, textures, finish and colours
- Card and board – a selection of varying qualities and sizes

Mark-makers
- Drawing pencils, ranging from HB to 8B
- Graphite sticks (preferably in painted 'sheaths') ranging from 2B to 8B
- Chalks and pastels – a range including oil pastels
- Pens – felt-tipped, handwriting, italic and bullet-ended, 'dipper' pens, foam-ended
- A range of coloured drawing inks
- Charcoal
- Crayons

Adhesives
- PVA
- Paper pastes – wallpaper, gluepens, 'spreader' types
- Spreaders – commercial type or lolly sticks, plastic knives
- Specialist adhesives to be obtained for particular work and used only under supervision

A checklist of classroom resources, page 10

Paints
- Powder paint
- Tempera blocks in a range of colours
- Readymix paint
- Watercolour sets
- Acrylic, poster and oils to be used occasionally under supervision

Suggested colours for all paints are white (twice as much as other colours); black; yellow – lemon and yellow ochre; red – crimson; blue – Prussian; brown – burnt umber; orange; green – emerald, viridian

Brushes
- Bristle – a variety of sizes and types, rounded, flat etc.
- Decorators' – a range from 1/2" – 4"
- Soft, nylon or hair – a range of sizes for delicate work 0 – 8
- Foam-ended painting sticks (these can be home made)

Sundries
- Mixing palettes (old plates) and water pots
- A range of natural objects, eg. shells, bones, plants, cones, stones
- A range of manufactured objects, eg. cogs, items in wood, plastic, glass, pottery
- A selection of posters, prints, books and postcards of different artists' work
- Needles and threads
- A range of textile pieces
- Scissors – including left-handed sort
- Craft knives – to be used strictly under supervision
- A computer plus suitable software for artwork
- Sponges
- String

Black and white, page 20

Self-assessment sheet, page 165   Name:

My work is titled
_____

It is about _____
_____

I have used _____
_____

You can see these ideas in my work
_____

It was hard to _____
_____

I really like _____
_____

I learned about _____
_____

172

Self-assessment sheet, page 165　　　Name:

In my picture

I used _____

I chose these materials because _____

_____

_____

I wanted to show these ideas _____

_____

I looked at the work of these

artists _____

_____

I am pleased with _____

_____

_____

I learned how to _____

_____

_____

Photocopiable pages　173

Self-assessment sheet, page 165 Name:

The title of my work is _____
_____

I chose to use the following materials _____
_____
_____

I based my work on these ideas _____
_____
_____
_____

I studied the work of _____
_____

I particularly liked_____
_____
_____

I found problems with _____
_____
_____

I solved them by _____
_____

I think my finished work _____
_____
_____
_____

I could develop it by_____

Self-assessment sheet, page 165

Name:

Looking at paintings – colour

What are the main colours the artist has used?

Does the background have different colours from those in the foreground?

Look for different shades of the same colour – what have they been used for?

Do any colours stand out from the rest?

Why do you think the artist chose to use these colours?

What is the mood of the picture?
(mysterious, calm, happy, frightening?)

How has the colour been used?
(small dots, blocks, thickly, thinly?)

Using paints, pastels or coloured pencils, draw small squares and fill them in with the colours used in the picture. Try to match them exactly.

Self-assessment sheet, page 165 Name:

Looking at pictures – portraits

Who is in the painting?

What can we tell about them from the picture?

Why do you think the portrait was painted?

When was the portrait painted?

How big was the picture?

Look at the clothes and jewellery. What interesting details can you see?

Look at the faces of the figures. How have the features been painted?

Look at the hair. What is the style? How has the hair been painted?

What do you think the figures want you to think about them?

Self-assessment sheet, page 165　　　　　　　　　　　　　　Name:

Looking at pictures – landscapes

What does the painting show?

Are there any buildings? What are they?

When was the painting made?

How has it been painted or made? (oil, watercolour, acrylic, collage, pastels etc.)

When was it painted?

How has the artist shown distance?

Are there any figures in the picture?

What is the weather like?

What time of year is it? How can you tell?

Why do you think the artist painted the picture?

What size was the original?

What colours has the artist chosen?

Why?

Photocopiable pages　177

Self-assessment sheet, page 165   Name:

Looking at pictures – original paintings

What medium has the artist used?

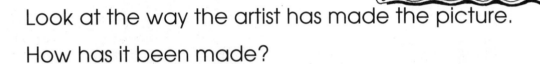

How big is the picture?

Look at the way the artist has made the picture.
How has it been made?

Look at the brush strokes. Are they all the same?
How has the artist used paint? How thickly is it used?

What is the subject of the picture?

What can you see in the picture? Look for details.

What did the artist want you to feel
when you look at the picture?

Shut your eyes. What things do you
remember especially about the picture?

178   Photocopiable pages

Self-assessment sheet, page 165   Name:

Looking at pictures – abstract pictures

What materials has the artist used?

How large is the picture?

What colours, shapes and textures can you see?

What is the title of the picture? Is it a suitable title?

What idea do you think the artist was trying to express?

How does the painting make you feel?

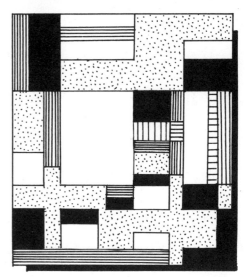

What might have given the artist ideas for the picture?

If the artist painted the same picture but used different colours, how might it have looked?

Self-assessment sheet, page 165   Name:

Looking at sculpture

What material is the sculpture made of?

Is it made from one piece of material or several?

What size is it?

What does it depict?

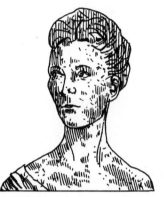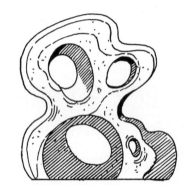

Walk slowly round the sculpture and stop frequently to look at it from different viewpoints. Sketch several different viewpoints as you take a walk round the sculpture. How does it change?

Look for signs of the artist's work. Can you find tool marks? Clay shapes? Drill holes? Unusual features and fixings?

Why do you think the sculptor wanted to make this sculpture?

What parts do you find particularly interesting?

Self-assessment sheet, page 165   Name:

Looking at textiles

How has the textile been made? Is it woven? Is it printed? Embroidered? Decorated?

What are the threads like?

Is the textile heavy or light, thick or thin? How many threads are there to one centimetre?

What was it made for?

Which country does it originate from?

What purposes can it be used for?

What colours have been used?

Could other colours have been used?

Could it be decorated? Embroidered? Painted?

Self-assessment sheet, page 165   Name:

Looking at artefacts

What material is it made of?

What size and shape is it?

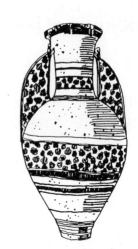

What interesting features does it have?

Is there any special decoration?

Is the colour significant or would any colour be acceptable?

What is it used for?

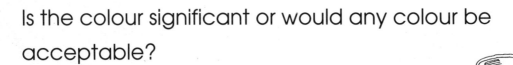

Is it well-designed for its use?

Is it attractive to look at?

Is it comfortable to use? Is it heavy or light? Fragile or robust?

Draw the artefact from more than one angle to make a visual record of it.

Pupil assessment and record sheet KS1, page 183

Name: _____   Year: _____

Key to completing boxes

◪ = some experience
☒ = growing confident
▣ = confident understanding

Attainment Target 1: Investigating and Making

Pupils record their ideas and feelings confidently and show a developing ability to represent what they see and touch. They choose resources and materials for their visual and tactile qualities to stimulate and develop ideas for their work. They work practically and imaginatively with materials, and techniques, and present their work in two and three dimensions.

Year
R 1 2

a (i)   Record observations from direct experience of the natural and made environments. ☐☐☐
   (ii) Record from what has been experienced. ☐☐☐
   (iii) Record from what has been imagined. ☐☐☐

b   Recognise images and artefacts and use them as sources of ideas for their work. ☐☐☐

c   Select and sort images and artefacts and use them as a basis for their work. ☐☐☐

d   Experiment with a range of materials, tools and techniques. ☐☐☐
    (drawing, painting, printmaking, collage, sculpture and textiles – see overleaf).

e (i)   Experiment with the visual elements to make images and artefacts. ☐☐☐
   (ii) Explore and recreate pattern and texture in natural and made forms. ☐☐☐
   (iii) Explore images using line and tone. ☐☐☐
   (iv) Explore colour-mixing from primary colours, and colour. ☐☐☐
   (v)   Explore the use of shape, form and space in images and artefacts. ☐☐☐
   (vi) Make three-dimensional work for a variety of purposes. ☐☐☐

f   Review what they have done and describe what they might change to develop their work. ☐☐☐

g   Know how to use tools and materials safely. ☐☐☐

Attainment Target 2: Knowledge and Understanding

Pupils describe and compare images and artefacts in simple terms. They recognise the differences in methods and approaches, use and make links with their own art, craft and design.

a   Identify in the school and the locality the work of artists, craftspeople and designers. ☐☐☐

Pupil assessment and record sheet KS1, page 184

Year
R 1 2

b Recognise visual elements (eg. pattern, texture, colour, line, tone, shape, form, space) in images and artefacts. ☐☐☐

c Look at differences and similarities in art, craft and design styles and traditions, from different times and places. ☐☐☐

d Respond to the ideas, methods or approaches used in different styles and traditions. ☐☐☐

e Describe works of art, craft and design in simple terms and explain what they think and feel about these. ☐☐☐

To be completed in discussion with the pupil.
I have used the following media:

Print ☐☐☐		Textiles ☐☐☐
Pencil ☐☐☐		Crayon ☐☐☐
Clay ☐☐☐		Paint ☐☐☐
Fibre Point ☐☐☐		Pastel ☐☐☐
Card ☐☐☐		Collage ☐☐☐
Sculpture ☐☐☐		Photography ☐☐☐
IT ☐☐☐		Other Media ☐☐☐

I have seen the work on the following artists, craftspeople and designers:

Western _____ ☐☐☐

_____ ☐☐☐

_____ ☐☐☐

_____ ☐☐☐

Non-Western _____ ☐☐☐

_____ ☐☐☐

_____ ☐☐☐

_____ ☐☐☐

I have worked:
   On my own ☐☐☐
   With others in a group ☐☐☐
   As a whole class ☐☐☐

I have worked:
   On a small scale ☐☐☐
   On a medium scale ☐☐☐
   On a large scale ☐☐☐

Pupil assessment and record sheet KS2, page 185

Name: _____   Year: _____

Key to completing boxes

◨ = some experience
◼ = growing confident
◼ = confident understanding

Attainment Target 1: Investigating and Making

Pupils record what they have experienced and imagined, expressing ideas and feelings confidently. They represent chosen features of the world around them with increasing accuracy and attention to detail. They select relevant resources and materials and experiment with ideas that are suggested by these. They experiment with, and show increasing control over, a range of materials, tools and techniques. They choose materials and methods and visual elements appropriate to their intentions, making images and artefacts for different purposes. They reflect on and adapt their work, identifying ways in which it can be developed and improved.

			Year 3 4 5 6
a	(i)	Develop skills for recording from direct experience and imagination.	☐ ☐ ☐ ☐
	(ii)	Develop skills for recording from imagination.	☐ ☐ ☐ ☐
	(iii)	Select and record images and ideas from first-hand observation.	☐ ☐ ☐ ☐
b		Use a sketch book to record observations and ideas and collect visual evidence and information.	☐ ☐ ☐ ☐
c		Experiment with ideas for their work suggested by visual and other source material.	☐ ☐ ☐ ☐
d		Experiment with and develop control of tools and techniques for drawing, painting, printmaking, collage, sculpture and a range of materials including textiles.	☐ ☐ ☐ ☐
e	(i)	Experiment with and use visual elements to make images and artefacts for different purposes.	☐ ☐ ☐ ☐
	(ii)	Experiment with pattern and texture.	☐ ☐ ☐ ☐
	(iii)	Experiment with colour mixing and use of colour.	☐ ☐ ☐ ☐
	(iv)	Experiment with different qualities of line and tone.	☐ ☐ ☐ ☐

Photocopiable pages

Pupil assessment and record sheet KS2, page 186

Year
3 4 5 6

f   Plan and make three-dimensional structures using various materials and for a variety of purposes. ☐☐☐☐

g   Know how to work safely. ☐☐☐☐

h   Reflect on and adapt work in the light of intention and consider future development. ☐☐☐☐

Attainment Target 2: Knowledge and Understanding

Pupils compare images and artefacts, using an art, craft and design vocabulary, and identify similarities and differences in methods and approaches. They begin to recognise how works of art, craft and design are affected by their purpose, including, where appropriate, the intentions of the artist, craftsperson or designer, and the time and place in which they are made. They evaluate their own and others' work in the light of what was intended.

a   Identify in the school and the locality the materials and methods used by artists, craftspeople and designers. ☐☐☐☐

b   Identify how visual elements (pattern, texture, colour, line, tone, shape, form and space) are used in images and artefacts for different purposes. ☐☐☐☐

c   Recognise ways in which works of art, craft and design reflect the time and place in which they are made. ☐☐☐☐

d   Compare some of the ideas and methods or approaches used in different styles and traditions. ☐☐☐☐

e   Express ideas and opinions, developing an art, craft and design vocabulary, and the ability to use knowledge to support views. ☐☐☐☐

Pupil assessment and record sheet KS2, page 187

To be completed by the pupil.

I have used the following media:

Print	☐☐☐	Textiles	☐☐☐
Pencil	☐☐☐	Crayon	☐☐☐
Clay	☐☐☐	Paint	☐☐☐
Fibre Point	☐☐☐	Pastel	☐☐☐
Card	☐☐☐	Collage	☐☐☐
Sculpture	☐☐☐	Photography	☐☐☐
IT	☐☐☐	Other Media	☐☐☐

I have seen the work on the following artists, craftspeople and designers:

Western _____ ☐☐☐

_____ ☐☐☐

_____ ☐☐☐

_____ ☐☐☐

Non-Western _____ ☐☐☐

_____ ☐☐☐

_____ ☐☐☐

_____ ☐☐☐

I have worked:
- On my own ☐☐☐
- With others in a group ☐☐☐
- As a whole class ☐☐☐

I have worked:
- On a small scale ☐☐☐
- On a medium scale ☐☐☐
- On a large scale ☐☐☐

GLOSSARY

The following terms are all commonly used in art and may well be encountered by the children in the course of their investigations. However, please bear in mind that the list is not comprehensive and the children should be encouraged to make full use of art dictionaries and other resources to expand their art vocabulary.

Aesthetics
The (study of the) theories of art and beauty.

Applied art
The application of aesthetic principles in applied design, furniture, design and industry, posters, cars, etc.

Appliqué
An embroidery technique in which pieces of fabric and/or other materials are attached to a background (usually fabric).

Armature
A metal structure used as a skeleton on which to model clay, plaster etc.

Artefact
A work of art produced by an artist, designer or other craftsperson.

Bas-relief
A sculpture in low relief.

Batik
A technique for decorating fabric in which a design is drawn with wax or another water-resistant substance before the cloth is dyed.

Biscuit
Ceramics after first firing.

Casting
The process of duplicating an original design.

Ceramics
Artefacts made from clay.

Classical
A term used to describe art that is either Greek or Roman, or influenced by Greek or Roman art in style.

Clay relief
Clay modelling in which the design stands out from the background.

Collage
A picture or design made from paper, fabric etc.

Composition
Arrangement of colour, shape, line in a work of art.

Diorama
Victorian revolving cylinder containing many pictures, which appear to move when the cylinder is in motion.

Diptych
An altar-piece consisting of two hinged panels.

Earth colours
Pigments (yellow, ochre, terra verte and umber) which are obtained by mining.

Enamelling
The process of applying vitreous substances of various colours to metallic or porcelain surfaces.

Firing
The process of baking pottery at high temperature in a special oven known as a kiln.

Fixative
A solution which can be sprayed, usually on to pencil or chalk drawings, to fix them and prevent smudging.

Form
The structural elements in a work.

Frottage
A technique invented by the Surrealist, Max Ernst. The process consists of taking rubbings from various surfaces. The results are used to stimulate the imagination and motivate ideas.

Genre
Group, style.

Glaze
A substance that can be used in the final stages of pottery to add lustre to a piece. Glazes can be bought ready-mixed or in powder form.

Icon
An eastern religious image, painting or mosaic of a sacred personage, which is itself regarded as sacred.

Iconography
The language of symbols, pictures and images. The representation of ideas etc. through a system of symbolic imagery.

Impasto
A painting technique in which paint is applied very thickly.

Impressionism
An art movement developed in France in the late nineteenth century. The Impressionists experimented with using dabs of paint to capture the changing effects of light on everyday places and people.

Line
A continuous mark that can take many directions, outline shapes and sizes.

Maquette
A model used by sculptors as a guide for a larger work.

Matt surface
A dull, flat surface, without gloss or sheen.

Medium
(Plural, media.) In general, the particular material with which work is executed: watercolour, oils, pencil, clay etc.

Mobile
A construction, usually suspended, with the property of movement.

Monochrome
A painting, print etc. in one colour.

Monotype
A method of taking prints off a sheet or piece of Formica.

Montage
A collection of similar materials, usually photographs or illustrations, arranged into an interesting design.

Motif
Simple design.

Palette
This not only refers to the surface on which painters set out their colours but also refers to the range of colours used. It can also refer to the group or school, like the Impressionists' palette.

Papier mâché
A modelling material made from torn pieces of paper soaked in paste and moulded into shape while still wet.

Perspective
The technique artists use to give a flat surface a three-dimensional appearance. Perspective was developed during the Renaissance.

Print
An image which can be repeated on various media, being transferred from a printing block of some kind.

Relief
Carving, moulding etc. in which the design stands out from the background. It can be high or low relief.

Renaissance
The revival of interest in classical art from the fourteenth to sixteenth century, mainly in Italy.

Resist
A technique for decorating paper, fabric, etc., based on the principle that certain substances, such as wax, are water-repellent and therefore paint or dye will remain only on the areas to which it has not been applied.

Sketch
A quick drawing, sculpture or painting as a first draft, before a more complete one is made.

Slip
Liquid clay, which can be coloured and used for decorating. It is also needed to join pieces of clay together.

Space
This refers to the depth of an object, rather than a flat two-dimensional picture. The technique of perspective can be used to create an illusion of space on a flat surface.

Squaring up
A method of enlarging a small design to a larger size by the division of both into a grid, then matching up the contents of both sets of squares.

Still life
An arrangement of inanimate objects – flowers, jugs, etc.

Study
A careful preliminary design for a proposed work.

Surrealism
A twentieth century movement in art using dream-like images to express the subconscious.

Textiles
The art of industry of designing and manufacturing cloths and fabrics.

Texture
Surface quality which is real or is suggested.

Triptych
Paintings, in the form of panels, generally three in number.

Vanishing point
In perspective, the point on the horizon at which parallel lines appear to vanish.

Wedging
The method used to prepare clay for use. It involves squeezing, rolling and throwing the clay on to a work surface to expel bubbles and to ensure that the clay is of an even consistency.

AT CHART

Scotland

The chart on this page shows the levels and strands for art and design in the Scottish Curriculum for Expressive Arts, 5–14.

Strand / Level	Investigating visually and recording	Using media	Using visual elements	Creating and designing	Communicating	Observing, reflecting, describing and responding
A	1/3, 1/4, 1/12, 8/2, 8/4, 8/5, 9/1, 10/2-5	1/1-3, 3/1-2, 3/5-6, 4/1, 5/1, 5/4-5, 8/2, 8/4-5, 10/2-5	1/1-4, 3/5, 4/1, 5/1, 5/4-5, 8/2, 8/4-5, 10/2-5	1/2, 3/5-6, 4/1, 5/1, 5/4-5, 8/2, 8/4-5, 10/2-5	1/2, 8/2	7/4-5, 8/2, 8/4-5, 9/1-3, 10/2-5
B	1/3-8, 1/11-12, 2/3, 2/5, 2/7-11, 5/8, 6/2-3, 7/1-3, 8/1-9, 9/1-2, 9/5-8, 10/2-5	1/1-3, 1/9, 2/1-4, 2/6-7, 2/11, 3/1-7, 4/1-4, 5/1-10, 6/1-4, 7/3, 8/1-9, 9/6-8, 10/2-5	1/1-9, 1/11, 2/1-5, 2/8-10, 3/5, 3/7, 4/1-4, 5/1-10, 6/1-3, 7/1-3, 8/1-9, 9/6-8, 10/2-5	1/5, 1/9-11, 2/4-5, 2/7, 3/4-7, 4/1-4, 5/1-10, 6/1-3, 7/1-6, 8/1-9, 9/6-8, 10/1-5	6/3, 8/2, 8/8, 9/4	1/7, 2/4, 2/8, 5/2-3, 5/7-8, 6/2-3, 7/1, 7/4-5, 8/1-9, 9/1-8, 10/1-5
C	1/3-8, 1/11-12, 2/3, 2/5, 2/7-11, 5/8, 6/2-3, 7/1-3, 8/1-9, 9/1-2, 9/5-8, 10/2-5	1/2-3, 1/9-10, 2/1-4, 2/6-7, 2/11, 3/1-7, 4/1-4, 5/1-10, 6/1-4, 7/3, 8/1-9, 9/7-8, 10/2-3	1/3-11, 2/1-5, 2/8-10, 3/5, 3/7, 4/1-4, 5/1-10, 6/1-3, 7/1-3, 8/1-5, 8/4-9, 9/6-8, 10/2-5	1/5, 1/9-11, 2/2-5, 2/7, 3/4-7, 4/1-4, 5/1-10, 6/1-3, 7/1-6, 8/1-9, 9/6-8, 10/1-5	6/3, 8/2, 8/8, 9/4	1/7, 2/4, 2/8, 5/2-3, 5/7-8, 6/2-3, 7/1, 7/4-5, 8/1-9, 9/1-8, 10/1-5
D	1/4-8, 1/11-12, 2/7-11, 5/8, 6/2-3, 7/1-3, 8/1-9, 9/1-2, 9/5-8, 10/2-5	1/9-10, 2/4, 2/6-7, 2/11, 3/3-7, 4/1-4, 5/1-3, 5/6-10, 6/1-4, 7/3, 8/1-9, 9/6-8, 10/2-3	1/4-11, 2/3-5, 2/8-10, 3/5, 3/7, 4/1-4, 5/1-3, 5/6-10, 6/1-3, 7/1-3, 8/1-9, 9/6-8, 10/2-5	1/9-11, 2/4-5, 3/4-7, 4/1-4, 5/1-3, 5/6-10, 6/1-3, 7/1-6, 8/1-9, 9/6-8, 10/1-5	6/3, 8/2, 8/8, 9/4	2/4, 2/8, 5/2, 5/3, 6/2-3, 7/1, 7/4-5, 8/5-9, 9/1-8, 10/1-5
E	1/5-8, 1/11-12, 8/3, 8/6-9, 9/1, 9/5-6, 10/2-5	3/7, 4/4, 5/2, 8/3, 8/6-9, 9/6, 10/2-3	1/11, 3/7, 4/4, 5/2, 7/2-3, 8/2-3, 8/6-9, 9/6, 10/2-5	3/7, 4/4, 5/2, 7/3, 8/2-3, 8/6-9, 9/6, 9/8, 10/1-5	8/8	2/8, 8/3, 8/7-9, 9/4-6, 9/8, 10/1-5

RESOURCES

Further reading

Adams, E. & Ward, C. *Art and the Built Environment: A teacher's approach* (1982, Longman)
Arneson, H. H. A. *A History of Modern Art* (out of print, Thames and Hudson)
Arts Council Exhibition Catalogues *Three Little Books about Sculpture: Flesh and stone; Sculpture's dance; Mind over matter* (out of print, 1983, South Bank Centre Publication Dept.) Available for view in the British Museum
Arts Council Exhibition Catalogues *Three Little Books about Painting: Light; Movement; Image* (out of print, 1983, South Bank Centre Publication Dept.) Available for view in the British Museum.
Chilvers, I. et al *The Oxford Dictionary of Art* (1988, OUP)
Compton, M. *Looking at Pictures in the Tate Gallery* (1979, Tate Gallery Publications Dept. Millbank, London SW1P 4RG)
Davies, M. *Get the Picture: Developing Visual Literacy in the Classroom* (1989, Development Education Centre, Birmingham)
Durbin, G., Morris, S. & Wilkinson, S. *A Teacher's Guide to Learning from Objects* (1990, English Heritage)
Forder, J. and E. *Hill Shepherd* (1989, Frank Peters Publishing)
Gombrich, E. H. *The Story of Art* (1989, Phaidon)
Lancaster (ed.) *Art, Craft & Design in the Primary School* (1987, NSEAD)
Kraus, R. *Portrait of a Forest* (1986, Constable)
Morris, S. *A Teacher's Guide to Using Portraits* (1989, English Heritage)
Read, H. *A Concise History of Modern Painting* (1975, Thames & Hudson)
Read, H. *A Concise History of Modern Sculpture* (1964, Thames & Hudson)
Rogers, L. R. *Relief Sculpture: The Appreciation of Art* (out of print, OUP)
Wiltshire, S. *Drawings* (1990, J. M. Dent & Son)

Ceramics

Bagg, G. *Beginner's Guide to Pottery* (out of print, Newnes)
Beck, C. *Stoneware Glazes* (1973, Isles House Publications)
Billington, D. M. *The Technique of Pottery* (1987, Batsford)
Cardew, M. *Pioneer Pottery* (1989, OUP)
Casson, M. *The Craft of the Potter* (1977, BBC)
Clarke, K. *Practical Pottery and Ceramics* (out of print, Studio Vista)
Flight, G. *Ceramics Manual: A Basic Guide to Pottery Making* (1988, Collins)
Green, D. *Understanding Pottery Glazes* (out of print, 1975, Faber & Faber)
ILEA, *Clay in the Classroom* (The Fulham Pottery)
Jolly, T. *Introducing Handbuilt Pottery* (out of print, Batsford)
Leach, B. *A Potter's Book* (1976, Faber & Faber)
Rhodes, D. *Clay and Glazes for the Potter* (1988, A. & C. Black)
Rhodes, D. *Stoneware and Porcelain* (out of print, Pitman Books)
Rogers, M. *Pottery and Porcelain: a Handbook* (out of print, A. & C. Black)
Winterburn, M. *The technique of Hand Built Pottery* (out of print, Mills & Boon)

Sculpture

Bazin, G. *The History of World Sculpture* (out of print, Studio Vista)
Clarke, G. & Cornock, S. *A Sculptor's Manual* (out of print, Studio Vista)
Giedion-Welcker, C. *Contemporary Sculpture* (out of print, Faber & Faber)
Hammacher, A. M. *Modern English Sculpture* (out of print, 1967, Thames & Hudson)
Mills, J. W. *The Techniques of Sculpture* (1985, Batsford)
Pope-Hennessy (ed.) *A History of Western Sculpture* (out of print, Michael Joseph)
Rich, J. C. *The Materials and Methods of Sculpture* (1989, Dover Publications)
Trier, E. *Form and Space* (out of print, 1968, Thames & Hudson)

General primary

De Bono, E. *Children Solving Problems* (out of print, Penguin)
Durbin, G., Morris, S. & Wilkinson, S. *A Teacher's Guide to Learning from Objects* (English Heritage)
Fine, A. *Anneli the Art Hater* (Mammoth)
Graham, J. & Jeffs, H. *Practical Guides: Art* (1993, Scholastic Ltd)
Jameson, K. *Junior School Art* (out of print, Studio Vista)
Jameson, K. *Pre School and*

Infant Art (out of print, Studio Vista)
Jannszczak, W. & McCleery, J. *Understanding Art* (1982, MacDonald)
Keightley, M. *Investigating Art: Practical guide for young people* (1984, Bell & Hyman)
Kenyon, P. & Reynolds, T. *Art policy guidance – a guide for schools on the preparation and compilation of policy statements, schemes of work and guidelines* (1994, Dudley LEA)
Lack, M. *Bright Ideas: Art* (1991, Scholastic Ltd)
Lowenfeld, V. & Lambert, B. *Creative Mental Growth* (1987, Collier Macmillan)
Mayhew, J. *Katie's Picture Show* (Orchard)
Morgan, M. *Art 4–11* (1988, Simon and Schuster)
Morgan, M. *Art in Practice* (1993, Nash Pollock)
Morris, S. *A Teacher's Guide to Using Portraits* (English Heritage)
Rodari, F. *A Weekend with Picasso* (Rizzoli, New York)
Rowswell, G. *Teaching Art in Primary Schools* (1983, Bell & Hyman)
Skira-Venturi, R. *A Weekend with Monet* (Rizzoli, New York)

Textiles

Butler, A. *Machine Stitches* (1976, Batsford)
Coleman, A. *Fabrics and Threads for School* (out of print, Batsford)
Dyrenforth, *The Techniques of Batik* (1985, Batsford)
Gray, J. *Canvas Work* (out of print, Batsford)
Gray, J. *Machine Embroidery* (out of print, Batsford)
Howard, C. *Embroidery and Colour* (out of print, Batsford)
Howard, C. *Inspiration for Embroidery* (1985, Batsford)
Hutton, H. *Textile Structures* (out of print, Batsford)
Kinsey, A. *Introducing Screen Printing* (out of print, Batsford)
Proud, N. *Introducing Textile Printing* (out of print, Batsford)
Rainey, S. R. *Wall Hangings: Designing with Fabric and Thread* (1973, Davis Publications Inc.)
Rainey, S. R. *Weaving without a Loom* (1977, Prentice Hall)
Samuel, E. *Introducing Batik* (out of print, Batsford)
Simpson & Weir *The Weaver's Craft* (out of print, Dryad)
Thurston, V. *The Use of Vegetable Dyes* (out of print, Dryad)
Tovey, J. *The Technique of Weaving* (out of print, Batsford)
Wickens, H. *Vegetable or Natural Dying in Wool* (booklet, Dryad)
Wilson, J. *Weaving is for Anyone* (out of print, Studio Vista)

Art and craft suppliers

Berol/Osmiroid Ltd, Oldmedow Road, King's Lynn, Norfolk PE30 4JR
Dryad, PO Box 38, Leicester LE1 9BU
Galt Educational, Brookfield Road, Cheadle, Cheshire SK3 2PN
Heron Educational Ltd, Carrwood House, Carrwood Road, Chesterfield, Derbyshire S41 9QB
Hope Education, Orb Mill, Huddersfield Road, Oldham, Lancashire OL4 2ST
LEGO UK Ltd, Ruthin Road, Wrexham, Clwyd LL13 7TQ
NES/Arnold, Ludlow Hill Road, West Bridgford, Nottingham NG2 6HD
Philip and Tacey Ltd, North Way, Andover, Hampshire S19 5BN
Philip Harris Ltd, Lynn Lane, Shenstone, Lichfield, Staffordshire WS14 0EE